Praise for *Bridging Two Realms*

"The wonderfully gifted and renowned psychic medium **John Holland**
*has written a comprehensive guidebook to help you understand
and develop your own intuitive abilities and mediumistic skills.*
Bridging Two Realms *is a very practical manual filled with beautiful
stories, techniques, and exercises. I highly recommend this book."*

— **Brian L. Weiss, M.D.**, author of *Many Lives, Many Masters*

*"This book is a tour de force! I imagine that those who have passed
over are clamoring for us to read it to know they truly do exist. They
want us to learn how to contact them — and this book shows us how.
There are so many things that I love about this book, but the thing
that stands out is that simply reading it opens a mystic gateway,
making it so much easier to reach loved ones on the Other-Side. The
veil becomes thinner, and the light of heaven shines more brightly in
your life. Your loved ones are truly just a thought away, and*
Bridging Two Realms *opens those heavenly gates."*

— **Denise Linn**, author of *Sacred Space*

*"*Bridging Two Realms *is a must-have for those looking to develop
their mediumistic abilities and connection to the Spiritual realms. The
book gives clear, sound information about the psychic and mediumistic
process of unfoldment.* **John Holland** *also introduces those who have
lost someone to their own soul-to-soul connection with their departed
loved ones, allowing us to maintain a new relationship with them
between two worlds. This is a wonderful reference guide you will
return to again and again. Masterfully done!"*

— **Rev. Janet Nohavec**, pastor of Journey Within Church
and author of *Where Two Worlds Meet*

*"*Bridging Two Realms *is one of the most thorough, grounded,
practical, and inspired guides into the subtle realms you will find
anywhere. If you yearn to make personal contact with those in the
Spirit World,* **John Holland**'s *book will gracefully open the door and
lead you across the veil with ease. It's a beautiful guide."*

— **Sonia Choquette**, author of *Ask Your Guides*

BRIDGING
—TWO—
REALMS

ALSO BY JOHN HOLLAND

Books

*Born Knowing: A Medium's
Journey—Accepting and
Embracing My Spiritual Gifts*

*Psychic Navigator: Harnessing
Your Inner Guidance*

101 Ways to Jump-start Your Intuition

*Power of the Soul: Inside
Wisdom for an Outside World*

*The Spirit Whisperer:
Chronicles of a Medium*

CD

*Awakening Your Psychic Strengths:
A Complete Program for Developing
Your Inner Guidance and Spiritual
Potential* (4-CD set)

Card Decks

The Psychic Tarot Oracle Deck

*The Psychic Tarot for
the Heart Oracle Deck*

*The Spirit Messages Daily
Guidance Oracle Deck*

Please visit:

Hay House USA: www.hayhouse.com®
Hay House Australia: www.hayhouse.com.au
Hay House UK: www.hayhouse.co.uk
Hay House India: www.hayhouse.co.in

John Holland's website: www.JohnHolland.com

———————

BRIDGING
—TWO—
REALMS

LEARN TO COMMUNICATE WITH YOUR LOVED ONES ON THE OTHER-SIDE

JOHN HOLLAND

HAY HOUSE LLC
Carlsbad, California • New York City
London • Sydney • New Delhi

Published in the United States by: Hay House LLC: www.hayhouse.com® • *Published in Australia by:* Hay House Australia Publishing Pty Ltd: www.hayhouse.com.au • *Published in the United Kingdom by:* Hay House UK Ltd: www.hayhouse.co.uk • *Published in India by:* Hay House Publishers (India) Pvt Ltd: www.hayhouse.co.in

John Holland's editor: Simon Steel
Cover design: Charles McStravick • *Interior design:* Pamela Homan

Library of Congress Cataloging-in-Publication Data

Names: Holland, John, date, author.
Title: Bridging two realms : learn to communicate with your loved ones on the other-side / John Holland.
Description: 1st edition. | Carlsbad : Hay House, Inc., 2018.
Identifiers: LCCN 2017054731 | ISBN 9781401950637 (tradepaper : alk. paper)
Subjects: LCSH: Mediums. | Spiritualism.
Classification: LCC BF1286 .H58 2018 | DDC 133.9/1--dc23 LC record available at https://lccn.loc.gov/2017054731

ISBN: 978-1-4019-5063-7

16 15 14 13 12 11 10 9 8 7
1st edition, February 2018

Printed in the United States of America

This product uses responsibly sourced papers and/or recycled materials. For more information, see www.hayhouse.com.

*This book is dedicated to: Spirit, to the mediums
past and present who have paved the way before me,
and to my students — may you always trust in knowing that
your Guides and Spirit Helpers will never let you down.*

CONTENTS

*There's a special language that transcends
time and space — a language that's not constrained
by the limitations of just words, but one that
consists of signs, symbols, energy, and thoughts.
This language can be heard and seen only
when you truly pay attention . . .
It is the language of Spirit.*

INTRODUCTION

There could be many reasons why you're drawn to this book — or perhaps synchronicity had a part to play, in that this book somehow found you!

It could be that you've suffered a loss and are mourning, and you're looking for words of comfort, hope, and inspiration. You're searching for answers and you desperately want to believe there's a Spirit World. You want to know if your loved one survived death and is safe and happy.

Equally, you might want to know if it's really possible to communicate with those on the Other-Side. Maybe you're trying to help yourself or someone else by acquiring knowledge of what happens after we leave this world.

Perhaps you're looking for answers after having had your own psychic experiences. Or perhaps something inside your soul is stirring and you're interested in learning how to have your own intimate connection with a higher source.

Whether you're a student of psychic studies or a medium, a believer or a skeptic, bereaved or simply curious, I have written this book with great care in order to provide you with innumerably valuable information, all in one book. It's my hope that this book is the beginning of you receiving some of the answers to the questions you may have been asking . . . possibly for a long time.

WHO I AM

I realize now that as a child I'd always had one foot in this world as well as one in the next. Even at an early age, I knew that I was the "different one" in the family! I was a sensitive child, born with psychic abilities that showed up quite early in my life. I just knew things that others didn't. I would know when relatives were ill, even if they lived in another state. I would let my parents know if we were going to have an unexpected visitor. Sometimes I would even know exactly what people were thinking. To cap it off, on some evenings when I'd lay awake in bed, I'd see "the Spirit People" walking through my bedroom. These were shadowy, yet illuminated figures with the kindest faces and a glow around them. From my first encounter with them, I knew they weren't there to scare me; in fact, they went out of their way to look at me warmly, or simply nod a quick hello. I didn't know who these people were, but I felt strangely comforted and protected by their presence.

To me, all this was perfectly normal. I was never really frightened because I was born with this unusual ability. So how could I be scared of something that has always been with me? As I grew up, I became more fascinated by the existence of what lay beyond the physical world than what was right in front of me. Even at a young age, I knew there was more to this life. I could see that there was another world, a place that most people weren't aware of. I found myself inextricably drawn to esoteric subjects on different religions, saints, angels, spirits, reincarnation, out-of-body travel, and magic. As a child, I would always be found curled up with my nose pressed to a book. I'd read everything and anything I could on these subjects.

Little did I know that I was somehow preparing myself to become a spiritual medium as well as a teacher, and that I'd end up helping thousands of people. Now, I devote much of my time and energy to educating the masses. Through my mediumship demonstrations, private readings, and workshops, I'm able to explain the intricacies and the mechanics of mediumship and the Spirit World from a place of humility, knowledge, and experience.

I find it helpful and beneficial with every mediumship demonstration I do to make sure I begin with a short, casual talk. I find that the audience enjoys them and finds them interesting. The talk consists of how I work, or I might tell a few stories of previous messages that I have given so that the audience is comfortable and understands what is about to happen. I also try to impart the spiritual philosophy that I was taught when I was developing my abilities. I do this for a couple of reasons: to educate them on the process, and so that those who don't get a message will at least go home with a little wisdom and inspiration that they could use in their own life.

I'll also often try to get the audience to laugh. Yes, I know losing someone isn't meant to be humorous; I, too, have suffered losses. I explain, however, that our loved ones want us to be happy and go on with our lives till we meet them again. Plus, when someone laughs, it relaxes them and helps to open the door to the Other-Side. Nothing gives me more joy than seeing a bereaved person smile and laugh a little; you can literally see the pain on their face slowly disappear. It might be the first time they let themselves feel and express the emotion of joy in days, weeks, or even months. This all helps to make the demonstration run smoothly.

Sometimes, spirits are waiting in line, impatient to grab my attention and desperate to talk to their loved ones in the audience. When it all comes together, the messages are often mesmerizing and beautiful to witness. Some even bring me to tears, especially when children are involved. These are tender, heartfelt, intimate moments for all.

In my first book, *Born Knowing*, which came out (unbelievably) 15 years ago in 2003, I shared the story of how I discovered, accepted, and developed my psychic gifts. Over the following years, I've published several more books and oracle card decks related to the topic. I have much to be grateful for as I've had the privilege to travel all over the world, lecturing and demonstrating my gift to audiences throughout the United States, England, Canada, and Australia. By demonstrating my mediumship, I've been able to help tens of thousands of people who've suffered a loss to heal and continue living their lives with peace. I've devoted my life to Spirit (which is also commonly referred to as God, Universe, and Source) and to teaching psychic development. I lecture on all aspects of spirituality and the power of the soul, showing people that it's possible to awaken the dormant psychic strengths that lie within us all.

AN INNER AND GLOBAL SHIFT

I believe that something has changed dramatically since the publication of my first book. I've noticed there's an *inner* shift occurring within people — even though the masses don't understand why. Metaphysical and esoteric subjects have always fascinated people, but now there's an even more *noticeable* wave of interest that's occurring. It's not just that there's a general heightened interest in spirituality, psychic subjects, and the afterlife, but also there's an extraordinary heightened awareness in the consciousness of humankind taking place around the world.

Not too long ago, people were content to simply go to an intuitive or a psychic for a reading in the hopes of attaining some needed guidance in their life. Others would reach out to mediums in the hopes of receiving a message from their loved ones and friends who have passed. Now, however, people now want *more*. They're challenging previously held perceptions and asking thought-provoking questions, such as:

"What are my loved ones doing now they've passed?"

"Can they still feel and hear my thoughts and prayers that I'm sending them?"

"Is the Spirit World somehow getting closer to our world?"

"I feel I am in touch with those on the Other-Side, so does that mean I'm a medium, too?"

"Why am I so sensitive lately, and what should I do about it?"

So, what's happening exactly in society? Could it be that we're still questioning the nature of our own existence and our own spirituality is coming more to the forefront in our lives? Is the spiritual energy within humankind quickening and evolving? In my opinion, there is, in fact, a dramatic shift in our consciousness that's occurring. I feel we are becoming more psychically sensitive to the physical world around us, the spiritual realms, and, of course, each other. We're all connected, and we as a race are somehow "spiritually awakening."

All of this was my inspiration for writing this book at this time. I wanted to impart as much information in one book to help as many people as possible. I wanted to help the bereaved to understand that there is life after physical death. I wanted to provide evidence of the Spirit World and what happens in those spiritual realms. I wanted to offer solace through the knowledge that your loved ones are just a thought away and you can still communicate with them. They're still close, and they often try to reach out to us to lend their love and support. They're there to lessen the fear when it's either your own or a loved one's turn to transition to the Other-Side.

WHAT YOU CAN EXPECT

In *Bridging Two Realms*, I want to share all my knowledge, drawing on my decades of personal experiences as well as many of the inspirational stories and real-life case studies from people who've touched my life. The book is filled with philosophical and spiritual beliefs that I resonate with. Combining everything I've heard and learned from Spirit People with all I've been taught, this book offers one of the clearest pictures anyone could have of the Spirit World. I hope that it helps you pursue the unfoldment of your own spiritual abilities safely and wisely.

I respect that this may be your first time reading a book of this nature, so for the purpose of this work in particular, I wanted to provide you, the reader, with an understanding of the definitions of the words *Spirit*, *spirit*, and *soul*. Throughout this book, I will refer to all three.

- *Spirit:* When used with an uppercase *S*, this word refers to God, the Divine Source, the Universe. A spark of Spirit dwells in us all; it is the life force, the vital energy, that animates all life.

- *spirit:* When used with a lowercase *s*, this word is meant to be defined as an individual who no longer has a physical body. This is one who dwells in the Spirit World.

- *soul:* This word is meant to be used interchangeably with the word *spirit* for the purposes of this book. But I also try to express that the soul is the real you — pure consciousness. It is the soul that reincarnates and holds within it all the different incarnations and memories of different lifetimes.

I've included and enhanced some material from my other books that people have told me were particularly useful. I feel that some areas of this book, especially the psychic and medium-ship training, have valuable information and are worth repeating, especially for all those who are actively discovering and exploring their own psychic and mediumistic potential. As I said, I know this may be someone's first time reading one of my books, and I wanted to include as much helpful information as I can for a more complete book of my teachings.

I hope this book delivers what you're seeking at this time, whether it's a new way of seeing, a new way of approaching life, or just the beginning of your own personal spiritual awakening. Ultimately, I hope that it provides confirmation that mediumship is not just about connecting to the Spirit World; it's just as much about helping and healing the living. Know that there are spiritual bridges that can be built to connect to your loved ones who have passed, as well as the most important bridge of all: the bridge to your own spirit.

Part I

THE SPIRIT WORLD

Chapter 1

YOUR REAL HOME

Heaven, Shangri-La, Paradise, Eternity, the Other-Side, and even *Upstairs* are just some of the names that are frequently used to refer to the Spirit World. Yet, for many of us, we rarely speak openly about this extraordinary and mysterious place. We might well retreat into the privacy of our own thoughts to ponder or imagine what this special place might be like. In these moments of quiet reflection comes the realization that, someday, we will come to know this place ourselves . . . again.

As a practicing spiritual medium, there's one overriding question that comes up time after time: "Where are my loved ones now that they've left this world . . . are they at peace?" It's a very profound question, which has an equally complex answer.

Before I answer that important question, I first try to help people understand that you're a soul that comes with a body — not a body that comes with a soul. You are a soul first. The soul is eternal and can never die or cease to exist. The soul is the *real* you, composed of pure consciousness. You were a soul long before you came into this plane of existence, and you'll be a soul long after you leave this body to return home . . . to the Spirit World.

People imagine and define the Spirit World in ways that range from ghostly to beautiful and ethereal. There are different views or explanations of the Spirit World, depending on your religious upbringing, faith, and social conditioning. Too many people are influenced by how fictional books, television shows, and movies overdramatize their portrayal of the Other-Side. However, we'll never *really* know what it's going to be like until we leave this Physical Plane and enter the spiritual planes for ourselves.

I truly believe that the Spirit World *is* our real home, and our loved ones who are there are no longer ill. They're no longer suffering or in pain. More importantly, they're whole, reunited with family and friends who have gone on before them. It's those of us that remain here who feel the pain after we lose someone, mourning the physical loss of someone we truly loved.

As humans, we expend a significant amount of time and energy trying to make sense and understand our own beliefs about life after death. There are so many philosophies, so many opinions, and so many ways to approach this delicate subject. The whole thought process can be challenging. It's really not possible for anyone to provide absolute definitive physical evidence of the very existence of a Spirit World, as it's beyond the sphere of this *physical* life.

However, there are more and more people coming forward with accounts of how they clinically died but were resuscitated and brought back to life. They return to this physical world with vivid memories and images of what they'd seen and experienced when they'd temporarily crossed over to the Other-Side. Many speak of sensations, such as feeling a detachment from their physical body, feelings of serenity, or even releasing the pains associated with lifelong medical conditions. These incidences are called near-death experiences (NDEs). (In Chapter 2, we'll discuss what we can learn from NDEs.)

When it comes to describing the Spirit World, I go by what I have studied and experienced as well as the information I've gleaned from the Spirit People, who tell me of their lives in the Spirit World. Even though I've been doing this work for a long time, I'm always fascinated when information is conveyed to me of their time back home in Spirit. It's a joy to hear about who they're with, their surroundings, and how they still see what's going on with their family and friends here in the physical world. It's always an honor and a privilege to act as a bridge between this realm and the next, and to share the knowledge that none of us are ever truly alone. Now let's take an in-depth look at what's on the Other-Side.

WHERE IS THE SPIRIT WORLD?

Have you ever seen someone praying or calling out to their loved one who has passed? It's quite common for you to see people with their hands firmly clasped together in prayer as they gaze up. Alternatively, they might just call out to them while looking toward the heavens. However, I believe that the Spirit World is not "up there" but right *here* where we are, all around us. It's not beyond the clouds or thousands of miles away in some far-off place; it's closer than you could ever possibly imagine.

Time also works differently in the Spirit World. Because we have analytical minds, living by set time measurements of 24 hours in a day and 60 minutes in each hour, we're governed by time itself. In fact, it's humans who developed the concept of linear time. Many people live in a constant state of worry that they're going to run out of time! It just goes to show how time plays such a significant part in our lives. Yet time has no meaning in the Spirit World; it is a place that's not bound by the limitations of time and space.

The Spirit World is not separated from earth by what we understand as conventional distance that can be measured in miles or kilometers. It's as much about definitions, in that I prefer to define that spiritual place known as the Other-Side as a different dimension, sphere, or realm.

Everything is made up of energy and vibrates at its own unique frequency, and the Spirit World is no different. The Spirit World vibrates at a much higher frequency than our own slower frequency, the one in which we exist in this third-dimensional plane of existence here on earth. Since the vibrational frequency level is so high in the Spirit World, we're unable to see into it using our physical eyes. The fact that it's invisible to most of us doesn't make it any less real. Some people have had rare glimpses of the Other-Side, including those who have spent years training themselves clairvoyantly, those who have the ability or experience of astral traveling, people who were born with a heightened perception, and those who have died and come back.

SPIRITUAL PLANES OF EXISTENCE

The Spirit World is composed of many planes of consciousness and rates of vibration. It cannot be found in a physical geographical location because it's all around us, with different states of consciousness interweaving and blending with our world.

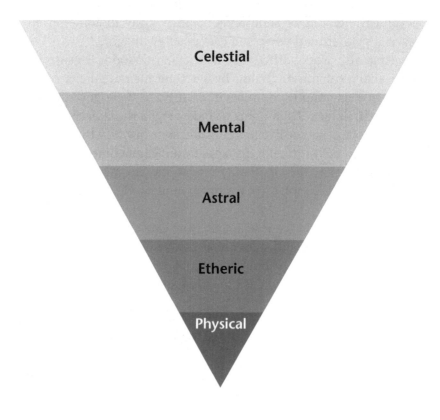

When we enter the Spirit World, we'll pass through these different planes. Each plane vibrates at a higher level, or plane, than the previous one.

Our own vibration increases incrementally as we move up to the next plane. I liken it to going up in an elevator, floor by floor, as we pass from one plane to another. The planes are arranged one on top of the other from the most dense vibrationally (Physical Plane) to the least dense vibrationally (Celestial Plane).

Below is the best explanation that I can give to help you understand the planes of existence and how this nonphysical universe works:

The *Physical Plane* is the bottom floor, here on earth where we all exist now. It is the densest of all the planes, where the molecular vibration is the slowest and where matter is about as solid as it is going to be. Events are ordered by time.

I know from working as a medium that those on the Other-Side have to lower their energy considerably to connect and communicate with mediums here. In order for me to communicate, I must raise my energy or vibration. This *quickening* process is as much a state of mind as it is a discipline, and it's taken me many years to perfect the process.

As those on the Other-Side lower their vibrational frequency and I raise mine, we meet halfway and their energy blends with mine, sending me thoughts, words, and feelings to pass on to their loved ones. Sometimes it's hard for me to maintain the link, so I have to really focus my mind and silence any extraneous mind chatter. I'm sure that it's equally challenging for those in Spirit to lower their energy for long periods of time as they communicate through a medium like me.

It's a strange feeling when the link starts to break down. They step back, and I can feel them slowly gravitating to their level. Using the analogy of a radio, it's as though the volume is being gradually turned down, or as though they step back into the elevator to go back up to their own floor.

Moving on to the next plane and decreasing in density brings us to the *Etheric Plane*. On this plane, time and space begin to loosen and become less consistent, which also makes this the start of the nonphysical world and the universe. Because of its close proximity to the Physical Plane, objects are still viewed as solid objects, and energy is limited to the speed of light. When we pass away, it's a relatively quick trip through this plane. Sometimes, however, people may stay in this plane a little longer, as if in a dream state, until they become more aware or awakened to their new existence of being back in the spiritual realms once again.

The *Astral Plane*, also known as the *Summerland*, is the next level. It's where we gravitate toward after death; ultimately, we will all go here. When I'm working as a medium and blending with Spirit, I believe that I communicate with loved ones who reach out from the Astral Plane.

This wondrous nonphysical level is filled with love, healing, and compassion. The Astral Plane is where we deal with any past hurts and other disappointments that were left unresolved while on earth. It's a chance to review how our life affected others, whether positively or negatively, and where healing and forgiveness should take place if needed. You're *never* alone here and will have plenty of family, friends, and guides to help you through your spiritual progression.

On rare occasions, some spirits can take a while to get to this plane — as if their elevator is paused between floors. I can see how a spirit may have a difficult time making their earthly transition, but it's my firm belief that there's help from those on the Other-Side to assist us as we transition to each plane of existence. Although there are people who have had their own experiences or have a different belief, in my more than 20 years of practicing as a medium, I have never personally experienced a "stuck" or "trapped" spirit here who cannot move on. I really feel that God, the Source, Spirit in all its glory, love and compassion would never let this happen.

Some people have asked my opinion about hauntings. While I've never been involved with or witnessed a haunting, I can see how a traumatic event could leave a psychic snapshot or emotion in the atmosphere, which ends up being replayed perpetually like a time loop or broken record. It's the emotion that's left over — not the spirit. I believe that hauntings are rare. If someone believes they're being haunted, it could very well be a loved one trying to get your attention. In my opinion, therefore, it's a visit — not a haunting.

The next higher planes of existence are the least dense, the *Mental* and finally the *Celestial Planes*. These planes lie beyond the astral and are so different than our world it is difficult to even comprehend what these planes are like in our own thinking minds.

Different faiths teach that the *Mental Plane* is a place where energy moves beyond the concept of speed, and objects and things do not stay in any one form. This is the plane where we gain the ability to move and subdivide our consciousness and be in many places at once.

Last is the *Celestial Plane*. Keeping to the elevator analogy, this plane would be the penthouse suite. Here is where energy has no pattern at all and is boundless in what it can do. People, objects, and things do not exist in what we know as form. Time and space are irrelevant here.

In some traditions and beliefs, this highest plane of existence is a state of God-consciousness, a place some may refer to as Heaven — the dwelling place of ascended masters, teachers, celestial beings, guides, and what are referred to as "angels" in some faiths. We can receive communication from some of these beings, even though they exist beyond the Astral Plane. They exist at a much higher level because they have been in the Spirit World longer and their progression has gone even further. I really believe that even though they are higher beings, they also never stop progressing on a spiritual level, just as we do.

IN OUR DREAMS

Did you know that many of us often visit the Spirit World when we sleep?

Our physical body can't exist without time to rest, regenerate, heal, and recharge our energy. Sleep is a vital function of our daily routine and overall well-being. Our spirit, I believe, also uses this time for a similar function. While we're asleep (usually during our deepest dream state), it detaches itself from its physical encasement (our body) to visit the Spirit World to regenerate. During this time, it's still connected to our physical body through what is known as the "silver cord," or "etheric cord."

Dreams are a beautiful way through which we can bridge this world and the next. Many people have reported having dreams in which they communicated with loved ones who have passed on. When we see our loved ones in this dreamlike state, it's usually just a fleeting visit. They appear younger, healthier, and more vibrant because in the Spirit World, that's how they *really* are!

As we awaken and the spirit returns to our body, we feel the connection start to slip away, as though we're letting go from an embrace. People tell me stories of how they often wake up with tears in their eyes as the feeling of that special visit slowly fades. I remember the first time it happened to me.

I waited a year for my mom to come through after she'd passed on. When she finally did, I remember waking up from this special dream with the distinctive memory of how we hugged in an all-too-familiar embrace. I could feel her love as though she had been right there with me. I still hold that feeling in my heart to this day.

Anyone who's seen my lectures and demonstrations will have heard me ask my audiences, "Who here has had a dream of a loved one, and who has had a hugging dream?" Usually, a sea of hands will fly up, along with nodding heads and smiles, confirming that they too have had a dream experience with a loved one. It's heartening to witness, and it just goes to further validate the existence of the Spirit World.

If the dream you've had of a loved one is a real visitation, then the dream is more than likely to be uplifting and happy. Alternatively, if you dreamt of someone experiencing sorrow or fear, then that's not a real after-death communication. More likely, you're still working through your bereavement. (In Chapter 4, we'll discuss what after-death communications are and how to recognize them.)

Trust me, you'll know a real visit when you have one. They're very healing and precious, and no one can take that away from you or say that it's your imagination playing tricks on you . . . or just wishful thinking! You know when these visits are true, as you'll feel it in your heart.

The good news is that we don't have to die to get a glimpse of the Spirit World. We truly can have connections to our loved ones who have crossed, even though we remain here.

THE THIN PLACE

Have you ever experienced being in a particular place where you've felt closer to God, Spirit, or Heaven? You just know there's something special about that place, and it feels as though it touches your very soul. The sense of peace and tranquility encompasses your whole being, and for some inexplicable reason you're drawn to this place, even though you don't truly know why. When you're there, it's almost as if the veil between this world and the next has been lifted, if only for a short time.

In the Celtic tradition, such places that provide an opening into the magnificence and glory of God and Spirit are called "Thin Places." There's a Celtic saying that Heaven and earth are only three feet apart, but in these Thin Places, the distance is even smaller.

Pastor and poet Sharlande Sledge provides an enlightening description:

"Thin places" the Celts call this space,
Both seen and unseen,
Where the door between this world
And the next is cracked open for a moment.
And the light is not all on the Other-Side.
God shaped space.
Holy.

Thin Places not only make us feel calm but also transform us, as if we're being unmasked. While we're at these places, we're aware that we're far more than just a physical being — we *feel* ourselves as a spiritual being, our true essential selves: body, mind, and soul. The Thin Places can be found anywhere on the planet, including churches, temples, beautiful landscapes, and ancient ruins. Any one of these places still calls out and attracts pilgrims today, whether located in nature or in the urban environment of a bustling city.

I've become aware of Thin Places through my work as a medium as well as through having felt the closeness to Spirit at a few Thin Places in various parts of the world. One place that stood out and touched me was New Orleans, Louisiana. When I was in my twenties, I traveled with a friend across the United States to move to California, and we stopped in a number of different locations. It was a time of great excitement, venturing out on our own for the first time. I didn't know what a Thin Place was then, but when I look back at that time, I firmly believe that I experienced my first Thin Place in New Orleans! I think it was a combination of everything combined — the history, architecture, people, landscape, food, and the wonderful music — that had the effect of making me feel closer to the Spirit World.

Another place where I felt a similar reaction was the Grand Canyon. When we pulled up to the rim of the canyon, we got out of the car to take in the magnificence and inarguable beauty that lay before us. There was no architecture, no bustling city landscape, no music or food — just pure natural beauty! It took my breath away, as I really did feel a sense of God around me.

Somehow, it seemed as though time stood still . . . even if it was just for a moment.

I'd be remiss not to mention one special place that I hold close to my heart. I can't explain why, but I'm drawn back to this place time after time; hopefully, I'll continue to visit for the rest of my life. It's a tiny coastal village called Trevone in the rugged county of Cornwall in the most southwestern tip of England. I can truly say there's nothing like it in the U.S., even though I've visited some of the beautiful fishing towns along the coast of Maine.

Trevone is nothing more than a cluster of houses around two lovely beaches, a place where you can see children playing in the sea, couples walking hand and hand, and elderly folks just taking in a little sunshine. It has sheltered coves and the highest, most unbelievable cliffs I've ever seen, with a natural blowhole formed from collapsed caves, where the waves force a column of spray hundreds of feet into the air! There's a walk that takes you on top of the cliffs, where you get to see the crashing Atlantic waves roll in one after the other, leaving your face covered in a fine salt spray. It's quite exhilarating and rejuvenating at the same time. Walking along these cliffs, I could feel that sense of thinness between this world and the next, as if I could literally step through the veil. It's an extraordinary place, one of spiritual energy. Every time I've ever walked there, it's been a special moment for me. Not only is it stunning, but also it's a time when I'll feel my mom draw close to me. The love I feel from her, as I think about the beautiful memories we shared when she visited me in the U.K., brings me to tears that quickly blend with the salty ocean spray.

Thin Places give us a chance to open ourselves up spiritually, to be present in the now and pay attention to the beauty that we see and feel. They are special places where we have the opportunity to let go of all the restrictions and burdens that separate us from communicating with God, Spirit, and our loved ones. I wanted to share these special memories here to inspire you, to encourage you . . . and to do nothing more than share something that's so beautiful and personal to me.

When you have a chance and some quality time for yourself, I invite you to think about or reflect on the Thin Places you've encountered along the way in your own life. Is there a special place that awakens and invigorates your spirit and opens the doorway to the Other-Side? Is there a place where you've felt closer to God, Spirit, or your loved ones?

Your special place can be revisited anytime you wish. Go there, not just physically, but with your imagination or when you meditate. Thin Places can be experienced once you learn to just open your eyes, ears, heart . . . and your soul.

WHAT'S ON THE OTHER-SIDE?

While people are usually afraid to leave this world, clearly there's a level of curiosity about knowing what's on the Other-Side *before* they get there. Lately, this topic is being brought up more and more often. My response to this line of inquiry is also in the form of a question, namely: Is it just curiosity or are they subconsciously preparing themselves on a spiritual level and don't yet know it?

Because we live here in the physical world, it's hard to comprehend or imagine what's on the Other-Side or what Spirit People may be doing now that they no longer have a physical body. Many people might envision ghostly figures, an eerie fog, or harp music echoing through the heavens. Life in the Spirit World is similar to this world, but far more amazing and vibrant. It's a world made up of wondrous scenery composed of beautiful gardens, rivers, mountains, oceans, and lakes. There is every animal you can imagine and cities filled with grand architectural structures. Everything is bathed in an extraordinary light, which is really gentle on your eyes.

I firmly believe that I had a fleeting glimpse of the Other-Side some years ago when I was writing one of my earlier books. While doing some background research into the fascinating subject of past lives, I had the honor of being regressed back to some of my previous lives by my colleague Dr. Brian Weiss.

Amazingly, during the regression, as I was floating above my own body, Dr. Weiss guided me to the *in-between place* — a realm that is neither in this lifetime nor one from the past. There's a feeling of total peace that comes over you when you're no longer attached to your physical body or your life. For a moment, in this extraordinary weightless state, I found myself in a world of Spirit, of pure energy. I got to witness the beautiful, vibrant colors that I'd heard so much about during all those messages I'd passed on from the Spirit World. It's true what people say: it's almost impossible to put it down in words. Nothing can really capture what I was feeling or seeing at that precise moment. When you think of it, how could I find meaningful and appropriate words to describe something that's spiritual and, in this case, nonphysical?

The closest thing I've seen to a depiction of the afterlife is from the movie *What Dreams May Come*. Made in 1998, this American fantasy film starred the wonderfully talented and now, sadly, late Robin Williams and was based on the 1978 novel of the same name, written by Richard Matheson. In the movie, the characters that have passed create their own special Heaven by the power of imagination and thought. Whatever they wanted to see or experience in their own personal Spirit World, they were able to manifest by simply thinking it into reality.

WHAT DO PEOPLE DO ON THE OTHER-SIDE?

What inspires us or motivates us here on earth also motivates us in Spirit. Whatever we loved doing while on the Physical Plane can be done, if we so choose, in the Spirit World.

As a medium, I've connected with loved ones in Spirit who've wanted me to relay some of the most touching messages about what they're doing on the Other-Side. In one such message, which took place at one of my intimate group readings, a young boy told me to tell his mom that he was out of his wheelchair, playing baseball and running the bases at a game. I remember his excitement connecting with me, as he knew he was talking to his mom again. He could barely get the words out fast enough, he was so excited to be telling her how he was doing all the things he was unable to do in his physical body.

As the message continued, his mom began to speak. You could hear the joy and excitement in her voice as she told me how her son had been born with spina bifida, a spinal cord defect, so he'd spent his entire life in a wheelchair. "He used to watch the other children in the neighborhood playing baseball in a field across the street from his bedroom window," she said. "Always yearning to be out there and wishing he was able to run and play like the others."

As the boy started to step back, I could feel his energy fade, but not before he was able to tell her one last time how much he loved her and was happy! It's messages like this that make the work I do all the more meaningful and worthwhile.

During another occasion, I had a grandmother come through to relay a message to her granddaughter. She described in detail how she was sitting on her porch, enjoying the sun in her favorite chair, which was the same thing she loved doing while alive on earth. The way she described it created such a clear picture in my mind. It was her way of validating exactly who she was so that I could connect with her granddaughter.

At a demonstration, I had a son come through to tell his parents that he was finishing school in the Spirit World. You could see the pleasure from his parents in the audience. The love between a parent and child is one of the deepest and most precious connections we make during our time on earth. Messages from children who've passed always touch my heart; it is an honor when I deliver them, as I know how much pain the parents must be in.

The couple stood bolt upright in the audience, tears in their eyes, confirming everything he was saying through me and telling him how proud they were to hear that he was finally finishing his schooling, which had been very important to him while he was here in the physical world.

One young girl came through to tell her family that she was teaching school to children in the Spirit World. It made sense to the family because when she passed, she had been just about to graduate with a teaching degree and start work at an elementary school.

I think it's important that parents and everyone know that life does go on in the Spirit World. You can choose to pursue what you loved on earth or try something different. Just know that your loved ones continue; death does not stop them from living, even though they're on the Other-Side.

Have no fear for your loved ones who have passed, as there's no illness, no pain, no suffering, and no more worries that are so often associated with the physical world, such as the need for money, mortgages, food, etc. In all the time that I've been practicing as a medium, I've never heard any mention of missing their homes or belongings. No one is upset over who got mom's diamond ring or other possessions. They've totally let go of the attachments to their earthly life and all things materialistic. They're at peace and enjoying being back home with their loved ones in their own private and unique Heaven.

WHAT OF HEAVEN AND HELL?

Many ancient cultures and faiths believe strongly in the concept of an afterlife, good and bad, Heaven and Hell. It is said that when you pass away and leave your physical body, your spirit will face the final judgment.

By the definitions of this belief system, it can be said that if you've led a good life here, then the gates of Heaven will usher you in. In contrast, if you're a bad person, then you'll descend and go to Hell. When we try to comprehend Heaven and Hell through our own human minds, faith, or beliefs, our visual representations for each generally place Heaven floating high above the earth in the celestial sky, whereas Hell is usually darker and found far below.

Even though I was raised as a Catholic, this whole concept *never* truly resonated with me. I can't relate to the idea of a devil who dwells deep within the bowels of the earth, surrounded by flames, where tortured souls are suffering. However, I think that most people in their own heart and soul believe that what you sow, you reap. Hence the saying, "What goes around, comes around."

I do believe that the way you lead your life, the way you treat others, and the compassion you show to others as well as yourself will ultimately influence and determine the plane you'll gravitate toward when you pass away. The kindness, love, and compassion you show will assist you in the progression of your own spiritual unfoldment, and help you become a better person both here as well as in the afterlife.

All the planes of existence are composed of thought, so in a way I believe we create our own Heaven or Hell. Whatever fate or judgment we have of ourselves is self-imposed. At the end of the day, we're our own artists and creators of our own unique world, as well as our own judge and jury. This is depicted in the movie I discussed, *What Dreams May Come*; the people who lived bad lives, didn't treat others well, or ended their own lives before their time are depicted as being stuck in a thick, mudlike substance. I interpreted this as showing that these souls who dwelled in this dark place were there as a result of their own self-judgment. In other words, they'd put themselves into their own temporary Hell.

However, I consider Heaven and Hell as states of mind, or consciousness, with Heaven vibrating at a higher rate as opposed to a so-called Hell at a lower vibrational level. There are many levels within each plane of existence, and every individual soul moves through them in their own time, at their own speed, when they're ready. It's not as though there's a penalty for overstaying at any one level; it's totally up to each soul.

Having talked to many people who had near-death experiences, I really believe what I've been told by them: Every soul, after it leaves its physical body, will go through a form of a "life review." In a life review, you get to experience and feel for yourself every joy, pain, and sorrow that you've caused other people in your lifetime. Ultimately, we all have to face up to our past mistakes. If everyone knew we would face this life review — where we are our own judge and jury — perhaps it would influence some of our behavior and choices in our lifetime, and make the world a better place. Healing, compassion, and forgiveness for others — as well as oneself — goes a long way when we speak of the soul's progression.

Let me just touch on the awkward question that's so often asked, "What happens to people who have done horrific things while here on earth?" Even people who are considered by many to be bad or evil have the opportunity to progress after a life review. They learn lessons as they experience everything they did to others for themselves. They probably incarnate many more times before they're ready to move to a higher vibration and through the planes of existence.

YOUR SPIRITUAL BODIES

In the same way that there are different planes of existence, we also have different spiritual bodies, as humans. We may not see them, but they're all interconnected with each other and constantly vibrating to their own unique frequency. From densest to highest vibration, these bodies are: the physical body, the etheric body, the astral body, the mental body, and the spiritual body.

Just like with the Physical Plane, the *physical body* is the lowest and the densest of all the bodies. The physical body is the anchor for your soul to experience things here in this physical realm.

The *etheric body*, which is very close to the physical body, provides the link between the physical body and the *astral body*. You can actually see the etheric body with your physical eyes. Imagine that you're listening to a speaker. As your eyes begin to relax, you may see a white glow around their body. It's not your eyes being tired or playing tricks on you; in reality, it's the speaker's etheric body you're seeing. You might also see a white glow around someone's physical body when trying to see their aura; this is the etheric body.

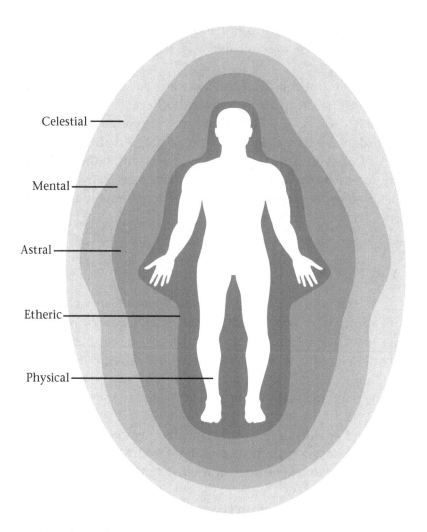

Celestial

Mental

Astral

Etheric

Physical

The etheric body is very important, as life-giving energy is drawn in through the etheric body and feeds the physical body with *prana*. It's the spark, or the part of the Divine Source, that's in every living thing, having a consciousness of its own. This spirit force is known as *chi* in Chinese, *prana* in Sanskrit, and *ti* or *ki* in Hawaiian.

If you ever see an energy worker healing someone, they're actually working on the etheric body of the person. Of course, there will be times when a medical doctor will be required to help you with a physical ailment. For example, if someone breaks a bone, a doctor may set a cast to help the bone repair. However, since you're a physical *and* a spiritual being, your etheric body will also be affected by the energetic imprint from the broken bone. In other words, what happens to the physical body affects the etheric body and vice versa. The etheric is not broken per se, but it's altered, and a spiritual healer can help align or clear any imprint in the etheric field, which will help bring the physical and the etheric body back into alignment.

Next is the *astral body*, which is said to be visible by some clairvoyants as an aura with flashing, swirling colors. The astral body is part of the Astral Plane, just as our physical body is part of the Physical Plane. This is the body that we'll inhabit after death. Many people have heard of or experienced out-of-body travel or astral projection. This is when the astral body detaches from the physical body and you float above yourself and can even look down at your own physical body. You might have seen pictures or drawings of a duplicate spiritual body suspended above someone's physical body. This is the astral body.

The higher bodies consist of the *mental* and *celestial bodies*, which are all connected to the higher and more evolved planes of existence. It's through the spiritual body of a medium that spirits communicate. There's a merging and blending of the bodies, which creates and opens up the bridge of communication between the two realms via the psychic senses, be it clairsentience (to feel), clairvoyance (to see), or clairaudience (to hear).

YOUR SPIRITUAL SELF: THE REAL YOU

As human beings, we host two bodies: the physical self and the spiritual self. The *real* you is your spiritual self — not the image you see in a mirror. Your spiritual self is what keeps you connected to your loved ones on the Other-Side. They are spirits, discarnate

— meaning not in the body. You're a spirit, being incarnate — in the body. Their passing doesn't sever the special link between the two of you; neither time nor space, and certainly not death, can ever separate us from those that have gone on before us.

People often ask me, "Why would I want to know or acknowledge the existence of my spiritual self as well as my physical self?" As I've said before, we're spiritual beings using a physical body to have human experiences. If you go through life denying yourself the experience of combining these two sides, you're missing out on so much of what life truly has to offer. When you fully integrate the physical with the spiritual, you can then start to lead a life of limitless potential and expand your consciousness.

We live in an age of materialism and technology; all too often, we're so focused on the outside world that we forget about our own spirit that dwells within us all. Many people who surround themselves with material possessions are under the false impression that doing so will bring them happiness, fulfillment, and a sense of purpose. Yet even when they acquire these things, they often find themselves asking, "Why do I still feel so empty inside?"

People who live a more spiritual life and who work from a spiritual level realize that there's *so* much more to this existence than what's on offer in the materialistic world. I've noticed that these individuals seem to get the bigger picture. They have a broader view and richer understanding and deeper respect of who they are, what they do, and how they conduct their lives. As a result, their connections to others here as well those on the Other-Side are more meaningful and special. Once you learn to lead a more spiritually enriched life, you'll be able to access all the unlimited resources that are available to each and every one of us. Once you begin to recognize that, you'll start to *feel, see,* and *experience* a world that you never thought possible.

When we become more aware and acknowledge the spiritual side of ourselves, then we can begin to tap into the greater part of who we are and, more importantly, who we're meant to be. This special, or *greater,* awareness helps us with guidance to follow our spiritual purpose of why we're here in this physical world at this time. It tries to give us guidance on the actions we take, our choices, and, of course, how we love and help each other with the precious time we have here.

Your spiritual self provides your physical self with insights and access to your intuition. It's the part of you that sends out that little nudge when it senses that you're about to make a wrong choice and urges you to reconsider. It's also the part of you that encourages you to help another person, an animal, or a cause. Often, you may be drawn to something, even if you can't figure out why. It could be something that you might never have been interested in or ever felt drawn to before. This is a perfect example of your spiritual self reaching out with intuitive or psychic emanations to guide you.

For example, imagine that you have a child who lives in another state or country, and you suddenly feel that you *have* to call them. When you do, they so needed you to call them. That's your spirit self reaching out and touching your child's spirit. Naturally, it's a two-way communication — spirit to spirit.

In my very first book, *Born Knowing*, I wrote about a time during my childhood when I was playing with some neighborhood kids in a schoolyard. Suddenly, for no apparent reason, I was drawn to a certain area where the janitors used to drive their trucks down a ramp to park under the school. It was as though I was being guided. As I looked down the ramp, I found a young man who had somehow fallen and was obviously badly hurt. I didn't even stop to think but immediately ran home to have my parents call for an ambulance.

Later that night, there was a loud knock at the door of my home, just as my family was sitting down for supper. I jumped up and opened the door to find a burly police officer standing there with a somber look on his face. He asked to see my parents, and I immediately worried that I was in trouble. It turned out that the officer was the uncle of the young man who had fallen.

"Your boy is a local hero!" the policeman told my incredulous parents, who were both staring at me with a look of pride in their eyes. "Sadly, my nephew's injuries were so severe that he passed away this evening. At least he wasn't alone — his entire family was with him and got to say good-bye." Putting his large hand on my shoulder, the teary-eyed man said, "Thank you, son."

It was a cruel twist of fate, but the injured young man's spirit had reached out to me that day, and my spirit had duly responded.

When we become more aware and acknowledge the spiritual side of ourselves, then we can begin to tap into the greater part of who we are and more importantly, who we're meant to be. This special, or *should I say greater* awareness, helps us with guidance to follow our spiritual purpose of why we're here in this physical world at this time. It tries to give us guidance on the actions we take as well as our choices, and of course how we love and help each other with the precious time we have here.

So, let me just remind you that we're so much more than physical beings. We are miraculous spiritual beings with unlimited potential!

Chapter 2

THE ULTIMATE
TRANSITION

There are two defining moments in everyone's physical lifetime, regardless of your religion, color, nationality, or geographical location: *birth* and *death*.

While they're totally different in the obvious way, I tend to view death as a form of birth. It's just that death is your doorway to the Other-Side, in that you're born back into the Spirit World.

Everything, including your soul, is *always* on its way to somewhere. The Chinese philosopher Lao Tzu once said, "Life and death are one thread, the same line viewed from different sides." Birth and death are basically the same process — it's like walking from one room to another through a doorway; in this case, the only difference is the direction you're headed.

A few years back, I heard a beautiful saying, which went something like this: "When a soul goes through the birth process, the souls on the Other-Side weep, while those on earth rejoice. When a soul goes through the death process, the family on earth mourns, while those on the Other-Side rejoice."

In all my years as a medium and linking with Spirit, I've never heard the people in Spirit say they were sad when a soul is born into this world. However, the saying certainly depicts the never-ending journey of the soul. From the time of our birth until the time we leave our physical body, we continue to grow, to learn, and, above all, to continually evolve.

THE PURPOSE OF REINCARNATION

It's important to know that throughout your lifetime, your soul absorbs *all* memories, feelings, and emotions, and your own unique personality gets firmly imprinted on it. It's only the physical body (your vessel), which is just an overcoat that actually dies. Once it's no longer needed, it's discarded like an old coat, and your soul (the *real* you) truly does goes on.

After the physical body passes, you have a choice to come back to this Physical Plane in another body to continue learning and growing as a soul. Being in a physical body on earth is the ultimate learning experience for the soul, because it's living through the constraints of the body and all the emotions and lessons that go with being here. Every decision and choice you've made in past lives, and especially those you're making in this present life, will influence your soul's journey in the future.

However, our lives aren't set in stone. We all come into life with free will and can choose to either move toward our purpose or away from it. We might plan to get from point A to point B in this lifetime, but there are many side roads and detours along the way that can easily take us away from our core mission while still encompassing equally important lessons.

I've had people ask me, "Why would a spirit choose to come into this life with all the pressures and conditions in the world, such as poverty, illness, strife, and suffering? It's almost unimaginable." When you're in the Spirit World, you become part of a God Consciousness, and as a result you understand *why* you're choosing to return. You also know that your time in the physical world is just a drop in the ocean of time in relation to your total existence. Someone who has what they believe to be a hard life will learn so much on a spiritual level as their soul progresses.

I often say that we should get a medal just for being here on earth because being *in* the body is not an easy thing! Our reward is the wisdom we gain throughout our time here on earth.

TRANSITIONING FROM THE SPIRIT WORLD TO THE PHYSICAL PLANE

It's not uncommon to wonder what exactly the spirit experiences during the transition from the Spirit World back to the Physical Plane when it's being reincarnated back into a new physical body. Lots of books and information have been written about the subject of death and the continuity of the soul. Many people ask me questions, such as: What does the spirit experience during this ultimate transition from the Spirit World back to the Earth Plane? Does the spirit enjoy and welcome the trip? Did they have the opportunity to choose the type of life they are being born into?

There's a lot of perceptions and knowledge of what happens after we pass, but when it comes to the soul's time to enter this Physical Plane, there's limited knowledge. I hope to answer these questions to the best of my ability with what I have studied, learned, and believe.

BIRTH: INCARNATING INTO THE BODY

If a spirit makes the decision to come back to an earthly life, then it can decide what kind of life it wants in its new incarnation. For example, it gets to choose which parents and family it'll be born into, although these choices are often contingent on the lessons it needs to learn.

Usually, when we choose to reincarnate, the memories, feelings, and emotions of our previous life slowly fade as new ones are formed, and we begin to live here again in the physical world. Yet some traits, skills, or mannerisms from our previous incarnations can remain. When I was a child, not only was I very sensitive due to my psychic abilities, but I also had an incredible talent for drawing. Was this talent inherited or was it carried over from a past life? I believe the latter. I also remember a friend having a reading from a clairvoyant once about his past lives. He has the most beautiful handwriting; he was told that in a past life he had been a scribe in a French monastery. It was fascinating, as he does have a natural way of mimicking a French accent, too!

There are many children who retain their memory of a previous life they lived. Some children have been retaining these memories since humankind began, but these days, it's become more accepted to talk about it. Some of the stories have been documented and even turned into movies.

One such story by Bruce and Andrea Leininger is one of the most compelling pieces of evidence about reincarnation that I've read. Their book, *Soul Survivor: The Reincarnation of a World War II Fighter Pilot*, gives fascinating insight into the experiences of their son, James. At just two years old, James was waking up screaming about being in a plane crash in 1945. He even remembered his name from that life: James Huston. (I find it amazing that they both shared the same first name.) Even though Bruce was a Christian, he came to believe James was the reincarnation of a World War II fighter pilot — a man who had been shot down over Japan in his plane and struggled to escape as it caught fire.

Through painstaking research carried out by James's parents, including interviews with James Huston's family and friends as well as WWII veterans, they were able to validate the information. By the time James was eight, the nightmares started to subside. Finally, James Huston's family was able to have closure after so many years. There's a lovely epitaph to this story, in that the Leiningers honored James Huston by making the long journey to Japan to place a bouquet of flowers at his ocean grave.

Some children have been able to describe a sense of being on the Other-Side. They recount how they chose their parents and share details of what conditions were like before they were born, such as descriptions of their parents' lives. These experiences are called pre-birth experiences (PBEs).

LETTING GO

As much as we might want to ignore the subject of our own mortality, many of us refuse to think about it, plan for it, or even accept it. Some people also feel that by just talking about death, they're somehow summoning it. Passing on — or transitioning, or whatever term you're most comfortable using — is something that we all have to face eventually, whether it's by coping with the loss of someone we love or preparing for our own passing.

Good-byes are never easy. Saying farewell to a loved one who's dying can be one of the hardest things you'll experience in this lifetime. No matter how ready you think you are, it's never easy when the time actually comes. If you're dealing with this at the moment, my heart goes out to you.

I lost my mother in the spring of 2011, and more recently I've also been supporting a number of friends who have lost loved ones. Even though as a psychic medium I know that we all go on and the soul is eternal, I still grieve loss just like anyone else. I know and understand what others are going through, and do my best to offer support and help.

When my mom went into long-term palliative care, I received a small booklet by Hank Dunn called *Hard Choices for Loving People*. This one little booklet helped me more than anything I could have imagined. It prepared me to cope with one of the most emotional and arduous times in my life! I share the following excerpt in the hope that you'll find some comfort in the words now or in the future:

> A natural response to the possibility of losing someone is to hold on tighter or to try to gain more control. Ironically, this does not lead to a life of freedom and joy, the very things we were pursuing. Most of us do learn to let go. We let go of our childhood and accept adult

responsibilities. We let go of our teenage children and our attempts to control them. We let go of finding happiness in possessions or careers. We even learn that we have to let go of other people and not be dependent on them for our happiness. To learn these lessons, we have to accept the fact that these things or people were gifts in the first place.

There are two ways to hold on. We can grasp tightly as we would a coin in our fist. We fear we will lose it, so we hold it tight. Indeed, if we open our hand palm down the coin falls from our possession, and we feel cheated. The other way to hold on is by opening our hand palm up. The coin may sit there, or it could be blown away or shaken out of our possession. But while it is there, we are privileged to have it. We hold on with an open hand. Our hand is relaxed and we experience freedom.

This small passage gave me comfort and bolstered my strength so I could get through those last months of my mom's life. I was lucky enough to spend a lot of time with her. As I perched beside her bedside, we laughed, cried, and shared stories and special memories. I made sure she had fresh flowers every week, arranged for her to have her hair done, and scheduled regular massages to ensure she felt cherished.

With a sense of openness and acceptance, we chatted about the end of her life, the Other-Side, and what to expect. I told her how those who have gone on before her would be there to welcome her home, so she wouldn't be alone on her journey. We talked about the signs she would send me, which to this day have been beautiful and heartfelt. I'm sharing one of the most personal moments in my life so I can get across what I believe is an important message: it's possible to accept an imminent passing with love and acceptance. I was able to enjoy my time with my mom while she was here instead of holding on tightly and refusing to let her go.

I'm not going to pretend that it was easy, but my mom lived the last part of her life with peace, dignity, and grace. She brought me into this world and held me with loving arms; in return, I held her in mine as she exited this world. I have no regrets because we said and did everything we needed to say and do.

Please say what you have to say to the people that are in your life now, so that you never have to say "I should have, could have, or would have . . ." or, "If only I had . . ." Try to live your life with an open hand, and enjoy and appreciate each and every moment you have with your loved ones, friends, and pets — for they are all part of your family.

THE GATHERING

If you know someone who's about to pass or who has recently passed on — whether it was a natural end-of-life passing or a sudden, unexpected passing — then I hope you'll take comfort in knowing that *no one* ever goes home alone. Those on the Other-Side are quite aware of an imminent passing and will gather together to welcome back a family member, friend, or even pet.

When someone is reaching the end of their natural life, a sense of peace often descends, as though they know that spirits are gathering to welcome them. When a person is approaching the final physical stages of what's known as *death*, they often experience a gradual declining or dulling of the physical senses. Their sight, their hearing, and even their sense of feeling seems to grow dimmer and dimmer. It's almost as if their light starts to fade or flicker.

When someone is close to passing, it's as if they are standing on the border of this world and the next. As their physical senses dim, their psychic senses get heightened, becoming more evident and acute. It's not so uncommon that the dying person seems to develop a sense of knowing or feeling of what's happening or occurring in another place, whether it's in another room or even a distant location. Their psychic senses — clairvoyance, clairsentience, or clairaudience — may become stronger prior to death.

SOUL-TO-SOUL CONNECTIONS

There have been documented cases where a person who was about to pass was able to project their spirit, whether consciously or unconsciously, to friends and family who weren't physically with them in the room. The loved ones were able to sense them and, in some cases, reported that they saw them! Others have documented how they appeared in dreams. You might have experienced this yourself with someone who was ill or close to death. It's as though you just *knew* you had to go see that person immediately, even if they passed soon after you arrived. It's almost as if their spirit was reaching out to you as a form of thought transference. The consciousness of the dying person is impressed upon the friend or relative even while the spirit of the latter remained in the body. I refer to this as a soul-to-soul connection.

This happened to my cousin many years ago when I lost an aunt to cancer. My mom was one of four girls, and one of her sisters, my aunt Shirley, was given the news that her life would be ending soon due to cancer. Everyone loved my aunt, and she was especially close with her niece Dolly, my cousin. One evening, while Dolly was relaxing at home with her family, she got this overwhelming sense out of the blue that she needed to rush to the hospital to be with our aunt Shirley, so she immediately dropped everything and jumped in her car. When Dolly arrived at the hospital, Shirley had already slipped into unconsciousness, and she passed peacefully afterward, holding Dolly's hand. It was as though she'd waited for her to arrive.

During a soul-to-soul connection, the soul or spirit reaches out with love and chooses a person to be there with them, or simply to say one last good-bye. You will often hear people say, "I felt them come to me just before they passed." The person who gets the signal is often one with heightened psychic sensitivity. However, I've heard many stories of how sad someone felt because they weren't able to be there for their loved one's passing. Some people have told me of agreements they'd made to be together at the time of someone's death, but alas it didn't happen.

If you had such an agreement that didn't work out, don't beat yourself up. You could have been at someone's bedside for a week, 24 hours a day, every day. Then the one time you go out to grab a coffee, your loved one passes. The person does not do so because they want to break your special agreement; the soul decides to leave so as not to put you through the pain of watching them go. They do this for one reason: they love you. The soul always knows when to leave or whether to stay and wait.

Even though I'm a psychic medium, I didn't get a spiritual message from my mom that she was about to pass. Instead, I received a phone call from my brother out of the blue. "Johnny, you need to get back as soon as you can!" he shouted and immediately hung up.

At the time, I was in Toronto doing an event with my publisher. By sheer luck, or maybe with some divine help, I was able to leave the same day and arrive just 90 minutes before my mom passed away. In those last few moments, I felt some of my deceased relatives draw close and felt their love gently surround us. It was comforting to know they were waiting to welcome her. Even though my mom was unconscious when I arrived, I believe her soul knew we were there.

I whispered in her ear, "Ma, all your family are here to take you home. It's okay, Ma, to go . . . We'll be all right. Don't forget that I'll always love you."

To this day, I firmly believe she *knew* she wasn't alone. A look of peace and tranquility had come over her face, and the strain of fighting for life had disappeared. As I sat there holding her hand, I felt her mom draw close, almost like when you feel someone stand behind you in line at the bank or post office. Then I felt her dad, her sister, and my sister all draw close from the Spirit World.

I said to my brothers with tears in my eyes, "Joe, Danny, put your hand on mom's heart; she's leaving now!"

My brother Joe, being a very practical man and a nurse, struggled to comprehend my words. He said, "What are you talking about?"

I whispered, "Joe, her family is all here. They're taking her right now!"

We all placed our hands gently over her heart. Time seemed to stand still at that moment, but within a minute we all felt her chest rise against our palms as she took her last breath and left this world. I'm sure that our touch, the strength of our combined love, and the gentle pull from the Other-Side helped her as she broke free from her physical body. It's a special memory that I'll never forget; I'll cherish and treasure it for the rest of my life. She didn't go home to the Spirit World alone. She walked hand in hand with her family.

DEATHBED VISIONS

Have you ever been with someone who's not long for this world and seen their eyes cast up as if they're gazing at something not physically there? Have you ever noticed a dying person reaching up with their hands as if some invisible hands were reaching back out to them? Have you ever witnessed them having a conversation with someone who's not there? When you ask who they were talking to, you might be surprised to find out they were having a conversation with someone who's no longer living!

This phenomenon is known as deathbed visions (DBVs), which some people experience just before they pass. It's less likely for such incidences to happen with a sudden passing and more common with a natural death or prolonged terminal illness.

Even my mom had a DBV toward the end of her life. One day, she was sitting up in her hospital bed, quite coherent, and said quite excitedly, "Johnny! Guess who came to see me today for a visit."

I started reeling off name after name of different people in her life that I could think of. All she kept saying was, "Nope, nope . . . Nope!" Finally, she blurted out, "Wayne came to visit!"

Wayne was her first love, who'd passed some 25 years ago.

"What did he want?" I asked her quietly, sitting down on the bed to hold her hand. She went on to tell me how she'd seen him sitting at the end of her bed in his sailor uniform, handsome and young like she remembered him. He told her that he was checking in on her to see how she was and that everything was going to be okay.

Examples of DBVs have been recognized and embraced by different cultures and faiths around the world, as well as thoroughly written about in both nonfiction and fiction. In 1926, the physician William Barrett wrote the book *Deathbed Visions* in which he detailed stories of people who'd experienced visions of deceased friends and relatives. He recorded how some had heard beautiful music, whereas others experienced visits from beings of light and angels. Barrett believed that these special visits were evidence of spirit communication.

Scientific study on this subject is also becoming more accepted. One such study, conducted by parapsychologists Karlis Osis and Erlendur Haraldsson between 1959 and 1973, reported that 50 percent of a population composed of tens of thousands of people interviewed in the United States and India had experienced deathbed visions.

Many scientists and medical professionals who feel they've had to offer a logical and rational explanation of such phenomena believe that these extraordinary experiences are due to hallucinogenic drugs or a lack of oxygen to the brain. I understand and respect that their opinions come from a place of education and rational thinking. But I would also pose the question: Why is it that these deathbed visions often involve seeing someone who's already passed as opposed to someone alive and close to the dying person?

Caregivers and medical staff at hospitals and hospices are also reporting more and more how their dying patients have talked about comforting visions or visits from a loved one. Of course, many of these experiences go unreported, as there's still a stigma attached. People are afraid of embarrassment, of being ridiculed or disbelieved.

After my mom died, I wanted to thank all the staff who had cared for her so diligently. In speaking with the nurses and aides, I was fascinated that many of them said they'd witnessed DBVs with their patients. I think that, knowing my profession, they felt comfortable opening up to me. I've found that people who work in the palliative care field often approach the idea of a visit from a deceased friend or loved one with understanding and care.

My colleague David Kessler is a grief expert who has worked in palliative care and studied with Dr. Elisabeth Kübler-Ross, the well-known psychiatrist and pioneer in near-death studies who gave us the theory of the five stages of grief. His fascinating book, *Visions, Trips, and Crowded Rooms*, describes the phenomenon of what people see before they pass. He deftly dispels many of the misconceptions and doubts surrounding DBVs and includes enlightening and revealing stories from a variety of sources.

One reason I love this book in particular is for the following story. David has kindly let me use this excerpt with the desire that it may dispel some of your doubts of this phenomenon. So, what happens when a person at the end stages of their life gets a visit from someone that, as far as everyone knew, was still alive?

A Family Affair: Heather's Story

I've worked in the medical field for years as a nurse. I try to know the ins and outs of the healthcare system, but nothing challenges a person as much as when his or her own family members become ill.

My mother, Mabel, and I were out on a Saturday afternoon. By the time we'd finished our errands and had driven back to my parents' house, it was almost nightfall. We were both surprised by the sudden darkness and then remembered that we'd just turned back the clocks the night before. As I brought in a grocery bag, I called out for my dad, Joseph, to hold the door open, but there was no response. My mother and I looked at each another, wondering what was up. I started to put away the food while Mom went to look for Dad, whom she was sure must be napping in front of the TV. She found the TV on, but no Joseph. She checked all the rooms and both the back and front yards, but he was nowhere to be found.

Mom called a few neighbors, who hadn't seen him. After an hour, we were both pretty panicked. At the age of 85, my father had stopped driving due to his failing eyesight, and we were afraid that he had attempted to drive. Although we were quickly relieved to see that the car was still in the garage, we couldn't imagine where he had gone or why. Our concern deepened when we saw his wallet sitting on the dresser.

Mother called the police, and I drove around the neighborhood searching. Four frantic hours later, we got a call that an officer had found my father across town, and that he seemed confused and wasn't sure where he was. The next few days were filled with doctors' appointments to confirm what we suspected, namely that Dad had Alzheimer's.

My mom, of course, had realized that her husband was getting older, but when she noticed the odd little things he did, she'd say, "No one in their 80s is a rocket scientist." Even so, she never expected him to wander away and forget where he lived. After the diagnosis, we found ways to make sure he was never alone and even replaced the locks so that you needed keys to get in and out of the house. Family and friends also pitched in during the day if my mom had to go out and I was working.

As if things weren't hard enough, my mother began to have stomach problems and was feeling very fatigued. Now I was dealing with two elderly parents in declining health. On top of my father having Alzheimer's, Mom was diagnosed with pancreatic cancer. I soon found that juggling my job as a nurse and caring for my own children as well as my ailing parents was more than I could handle and quitting work wasn't an option. My co-workers had been mentioning for a while that perhaps it was time to put my dad in a facility; and even though I'd resisted the idea at first, it now seemed like my options were dwindling.

So, my parents and I began looking at nursing homes and found Sunset Gardens, which was a really nice place. Dad was content, as this facility had a perfect mixture of comfort and security. After all, he was still a strong man in otherwise good health. It was a blessing that the move was surprisingly uneventful. Mom was more upset about living apart from her husband, so when she wasn't at her own doctors' appointments, she was there at Sunset Gardens with him.

At 81 years old, my mother decided not to undergo chemo or other aggressive treatments, preferring to let nature take its course. The doctors told her that she probably had a year or so, but no one expected her to suddenly fall on the way to the bathroom one day and break her hip. After a lengthy hospital stay, *she* now required around-the-clock care. Since her needs were different from my dad's, however, she ended up in a separate facility. I was now shuttling between my kids' school, my job, and two nursing homes.

For my mom, things quickly went from bad to worse. After the broken hip came a urinary-tract infection, then a respiratory infection. As her illnesses escalated, I was getting over to see my father less and less. Other family members would make sure he had a visit at least two or three times a week, even though at this point he was no longer recognizing loved ones.

Mom's doctors sat the rest of the family and me down and explained that there were just too many things going wrong with her body at once, yet returning to the hospital for more testing didn't make sense. While we agreed, we ultimately left the decision to Mom. She said, "I've lived over eight decades. I can't complain too much—it's just my time."

I was searching for a way for my parents to be together, but my mother's facility didn't accept Alzheimer's patients, while my father's *only* accepted patients with Alzheimer's and dementia. We were unsure if we should even tell him how bad Mom was doing because there was basically nothing he could do. We'd hoped to find a way to get him out for a few hours to see his wife when the call came that Mom's condition had worsened. Her blood pressure was dropping, and her heart rate was increasing.

That evening, my family and I sat by my mom, who was still very alert, but her breathing was more audible than usual. She suddenly looked up and said, "Joseph died. Why didn't anyone tell me this?"

I jumped in and quickly corrected her, "Mom, Daddy isn't dead. He's still in the nursing home."

Startled by her statement, I suddenly realized that I'd better find a way to get Dad over here. We were afraid that my mom was beginning to lose her faculties, and we wanted her to see her husband while she could still talk to him.

"Mom," I said, "we'll see if the nursing home will let us pick up Dad so he can visit." I nodded to my cousin Jackie to call the nursing home to make arrangements for one of us to get him.

"Joseph already came to say good-bye," Mom insisted, "and he told me that I'd be with him soon."

We all just looked at each other, acknowledging that my mother was hallucinating. I gently repeated, "Mom, Dad is in the nursing home. We're going to bring him here."

Once again, she repeated, "No, he's dead," but this time she also sat up. "Look, there he is!" She seemed to be gazing past everybody, and then she said, "Joseph, you came back for me." Her eyes filled with tears, and she lay back on the bed.

Just then, a nurse and my cousin motioned for me to come over and talk to them at the nurses' station. I met them just outside the door when Jackie said, "Heather, I don't know how to tell you this. I called the nursing home, and Joseph died about 15 minutes ago. He had a heart attack."

Mom died two days later. Even though I hadn't seen the vision of my father, I found great comfort in the fact that he had come to my mother, and now they were together again. Since my parents are gone, I rarely tell this story, but it feels as if I went from a medical nightmare to the universe stepping in, allowing Mom and Dad to pass away peacefully with each other. I admit that it's beyond my understanding, but I believe I had a special glimpse into a world rarely seen.

I often say that no one ever goes home alone, and I believe that DBVs show enough evidence for this to be true. Whether our passing is slow or sudden, surprising or expected, there's always a loved one to reach out and escort us back home. These experiences often help calm dying patients by lessening the fear of death. They can be extremely healing to the family and friends that remain after their loved one has passed.

If you know someone is close to passing, and they start to talk about someone visiting, the best advice I can give is to ask them questions about the visit — then listen with an open mind. You might be quite surprised by who showed up!

Hopefully, as the phenomenon of DBVs becomes more widely written about and accepted, it will assist us in recognizing that death is nothing to be afraid of. Most important, I hope that these stories and this book just endorse everything I often say — that you should live your life in the here and now to the very fullest. After all, this life is important. Life is fleeting, and every moment we fritter away is a moment we will never get back.

NEAR-DEATH EXPERIENCES

Philosopher, physician, and author Dr. Raymond Moody is referred to as the father of near-death studies by the *New York Times*. He's the one who coined the term *near-death experience* (NDE) in his seminal 1975 book on the topic, *Life After Life*. His amazing and in-depth research brought the subject of what happens when you die to the public.

Raymond is one of the most brilliant men I've had the pleasure to work with over the years. His wit, education, and knowledge — even his skepticism and scientific mind — just make him more captivating to listen to. His well-researched case studies chronicle interviews with people who've passed and come back to recount their near-death experiences. These real-life accounts must surely have helped many change the way we think about life and death.

People who have clinically died and returned to life have described their experiences of leaving their physical bodies and witnessing their spirits floating above their bodies. They could clearly see what was happening below them, such as doctors and nurses working away, or even what was happening in another room or place. In their stories, they talk about feeling a sense of weightlessness and being released from the pain. At the actual time of death, they say they felt a sense of release. As they look down at their physical bodies, they know it's theirs, but in a strange way, they no longer feel emotionally or consciously attached to it.

They rarely talk about how it felt to be dead but instead focus on the feelings of being more alive than ever! Their senses become amplified, their hearing and sight heightened. They're aware of having a body that is similar to their physical body but somehow made up of a finer, more transparent material. What they're seeing is their spirit body — a body that's no longer in pain, one that's not constrained by time and space as it moves freely to wherever it's drawn.

There are many stories about entering a tunnel of light where those who have passed are met by loved ones, family, friends, and even pets that have passed on before them. Others talk of being welcomed by beings of light. They describe a place of beauty beyond their wildest comprehension and a sense of peace and unconditional love. As much as they might love being there, in some NDEs they're told they can't stay and must go back because it's not their time. Other people have experienced an NDE in which they do get to choose whether to stay or come back to the physical realm.

These NDEs have been happening since the beginning of mankind, but more and more people are now coming forward to tell their stories. When someone dies and comes back, they tell of how shocked and surprised they were to find themselves back in their body. But they now look at life in a whole new way and seem to have more love and compassion for others and themselves. The majority of those who've had this experience also say how they no longer fear death and are able to make dramatic changes to their lives.

As I mentioned, some scientists argue that this phenomenon is caused by the brain reacting to a lack of oxygen, medication, or other biochemical changes due to dying. However, this doesn't explain the NDEs in which people can describe things happening in another room. Several of Dr. Moody's cases describe people who see or hear their loved ones in the waiting room or in the chapel of the hospital. When they come back to their bodies after being resuscitated, they are able to offer detailed accounts of exactly what they saw or heard, which can then be verified by their loved ones.

SHARED-DEATH EXPERIENCES

Dr. Moody was the first to study and write about shared-death experiences (SDEs) in his 2010 book, *Glimpses of Eternity*. In this profound occurrence, a family member, friend, bystander, or unrelated health-care worker or caregiver gets to experience the initial transition of the dying person passing from this world to the next. Interestingly, none of the "rational" explanations for an

NDE apply to an SDE because these bystanders are neither med-icated nor dying and unlikely to be hallucinating. Dr. Moody believes that SDEs present the most compelling evidence to date of the existence of an afterlife.

Dr. Moody had his own SDE in 1994 when he and his siblings gathered around his dying mother's bedside. At the time of her death, they had extraordinary joint and individual experiences. They all felt a strong pull upward, and the light in the room grew soft and fuzzy. He experienced the whole configuration of the room change shape. His sister saw their father coming to collect their mother. Instead of sadness, the dominant feeling of the room became one of joy.

Details can be remarkably similar among SDEs, NDEs, and DBVs, although no two are identical and every person may expe-rience something different. Documented SDEs typically include one or more of the following:

- Seeing changes in the shape of a room
- Hearing beautiful or celestial music
- Viewing the spirit or mist rising from the dying person's body
- Sharing an out-of-body experience
- Feeling a strong pull upward on the body
- Being engulfed in a brilliant, loving light
- Sharing in the life review of the dying person
- Accompanying the person partially through the tunnel
- Being greeted by deceased relatives and friends
- Encountering heavenly realms and dimensions
- Feeling a sense of being pulled back to the normal present

People who go through an SDE also have a greater appreciation for life and no longer fear death. The experience often alters their beliefs in an afterlife. Those who go through an SDE may find that their grief is dramatically reduced. Even though they still mourn, they feel comfort in knowing that their loved one is well in the Spirit World — and they'll definitely see them again.

Chapter 3

GRIEVING TO BELIEVING

In an ideal world, loving someone would not bring a heavy heart, sadness, or pain. Yet in *our* world, the reality is undeniable. At some time or another in our lives, we'll all experience one of the hardest of losses: the passing of someone we love.

THE PROCESS OF GRIEVING

No matter whom you've lost — whether it's a grandparent, parent, spouse or partner, a child, a friend, co-worker, or even a beloved pet — there's no way of getting around the fact that you need to work through the grieving process of losing someone as well as the pain that's associated with that loss. Grief can affect us physically, emotional, mentally, and spiritually. It is a uniquely personal experience for each of us, and there are no set rules as to how you should respond. Many factors can affect your personal experience of grief, such as your personality, life experiences, coping skills, and faith.

How you cope with loss often depends on the circumstances of the death. If it's the sudden loss of someone you love and were close to, then it might feel as if there's a gaping hole in your life; there's a raw feeling that you never had enough time to say good-bye. With a long-term illness, even though you have to watch your loved one suffer, there's often time to talk, to say all those little things that are so important. Then, when they eventually pass, you may feel guilt coupled with relief that your loved one is no longer in pain. Please know that these types of emotions are totally normal; no one wants to see anyone they care about suffer, especially when taking into account that their dignity, their sense of independence, and their personal identity are at stake.

I deal with both sudden and expected loss with the work I do. All too often, people come to me with the usual list of unanswered questions:

"Did I say enough? Did I do enough?"
"Do they know how much I love them?"
"Can I fulfill the dreams we had on my own now?"
"Where was God?"
"Am I strong enough to get through this?"

People tell me of their loneliness and of their aching hearts, saying it's all too much and more than they can bear. As the reality of becoming an "I" rather than a "we" dawns, immediate challenges need to be faced, such as how to manage the finances and bring up the children or grandchildren. Then, coupled with the practical stresses, there's often anger at the universe or a loss of faith in a higher power. Again, these are natural responses to grief. It doesn't matter how old you are or how long you were able to share your life with your loved one, it's perfectly okay to feel such strength and depth of emotion.

You'll likely experience many emotions after a loss, including shock, anger, guilt, and sadness. If you feel overwhelmed by your feelings and worry that they'll never fade or disappear, try to remember that it's all quite natural. Learning to accept these feelings, and letting yourself *feel* what you're feeling, is an essential stage of the healing process.

As everyone grieves individually and differently, you may experience any number of the symptoms of grief, such as feeling physically drained, being unable to sleep, being forgetful, diminished appetite, overindulging with food and drink, or throwing yourself into work as a way to avoid dealing with the grief. Some people can become withdrawn and lonely, experiencing frequent crying spells or walking around in a dreamlike trance.

There's no set time period for healing; everyone sets their own pace. It cannot be hurried, controlled, or even forced. Healing for some people can happen in just weeks, whereas for others it can take months or even years. Some people feel that if they let go of the bereavement, then it's as though they're totally letting go of the one they loved. Please know that this is not the case. Bereavement is something that we're *not* meant to hold on to.

If the grief is still very heavy after six months, and you're struggling to enjoy a reasonable quality of life while neglecting other important areas in your life, then I recommend seeking the assistance of a professional bereavement counselor or therapist. There is absolutely nothing wrong in reaching out for help. Sometimes our families or dearest friends are unable to offer the necessary counsel to ease our pain.

There are times when life deals us such a severe blow that healing doesn't seem like it is ever going to be a possibility. There's no way to avoid the pain of losing someone, but there *is* a way to navigate through it. Be gentle with yourself. Be patient and find the solution that works best for *you* on your terms, at your speed. After a period of mourning the loss, the pain will start to ease as acceptance slowly takes over. Eventually, joy and hope slowly start to emerge, day by day. You'll notice how you're able to talk about your passed loved one instead of having your memories consuming your thoughts and overwhelming you. You'll feel a sense of aliveness for yourself as you begin to emerge and learn to stand on your own — with your loved one standing right beside you.

BELIEVING IN THE AFTERLIFE

Belief in the afterlife is not necessarily automatic. One of the most poignant questions that some people ask themselves at some point in their lives is: "Will I live after death?"

When someone loses a loved one to death, millions of people all over the world ask questions such as:

"Is there really an afterlife?"
"Is it my imagination that I feel them still with me?"
"Are they the same person as they were here?"
"Do they know how much I miss them?"

It's these questions and more that truly validate why mediumship makes such a profound contribution with irrefutable evidence that life *does* continue when the physical body ends its existence.

Many people experience messages from spirit, even though they can be so subtle. You may not notice them initially, especially if you're still grieving the loss of a loved one. You might even convince yourself that something couldn't possibly be a message and put it down to coincidence.

I do want to remind you, however, that your loved ones want to help with your grief. They want to let you know that they're still a big part of your life. It's their way of saying that they'll be with you during the bad times — as well as the good ones. When you become more aware of the connection, it can bring great comfort to know they're with you during those birthdays, cookouts, anniversary parties, and family celebrations. They take such joy in attending and revel in the feeling of love from those still here. Love is a powerful force; it draws them close and assists in building the bridge between the two realms.

When you adopt the belief or awareness that your soul doesn't die and your spirit lives on, you'll draw strength and reassurance as *your people* on the Other-Side draw close from time to time, especially when you need support the most. Just because they're not here physically doesn't mean they're not with you spiritually.

During my mediumship demonstrations, I always explain to my audience that I can't *prove* there is a definitive afterlife! We'll know when we get there that's it's real. It brings to mind the famous saying: "I'll believe it when I see it." Some clever person turned the words around to create a whole new meaning: "You'll see it when you believe it." (I feel it makes more sense this way!)

As a medium, I know that I can only give the best possible evidence that I receive to confirm that our loved ones are alive and well in the Spirit World. My goal is for just one person to leave one of my demonstrations, saying, "How could he know such intimate facts that only myself and my loved one shared?" I want at least one person to feel inspired to do their own research about the subject. If one person is helped in their bereavement, if someone is in less pain or I've opened a door to the possibility that there really is an afterlife . . . then I feel I've done my job.

I've given thousands of messages over the years, but the following is one I'm unlikely to ever forget. I call stories like this my "keepers." The story concerns a boy who passed tragically and a mother who had missed him so much for a very long time. Every so often, those on the Other-Side make a little extra effort to help someone here come to terms and believe that there really is an afterlife.

Sunflowers for Mother

They say that every flower is a smile from Heaven; on this day, someone was about to get a special delivery! A few years ago, I did a demonstration in Seattle, Washington, at one of Hay House's I Can Do It conferences. Before the event, I was taking a stroll along one of Seattle's most famous landmarks, the boardwalk of Pike Place Market. Everyone was enjoying the beautiful weather, and the air was filled with a clamor of noises, tantalizing smells, and vibrant colors. The market was filled with vendors, artists, music, shops of all kinds, and packed restaurants.

As I was admiring the many different styles of floral arrangements, a certain bouquet of sunflowers drew my attention. I couldn't take my eyes off them. I stood there for a moment, wondering why I was drawn to them. Yes, I loved the majesty and color of sunflowers, but I knew I wasn't about to buy them just to take home on the plane the next day! Still, I just felt this overwhelming urge to buy them. It was a clear signal and a gentle nudge from Heaven.

Over the years, I've learned that it's best to just go with my gut at times like these. Someone on the Other-Side clearly wanted me to buy some sunflowers. I've gotten signs like this many times before, although instead of a flower it might be a a crystal, a picture, or some other special memento. Every time, I'll later learn of the specific meaning the gift has to the person who will receive it. You see, the gift is not really from me. I'm just inspired to purchase it, while trusting that it will make its way to the right recipient.

Of course, I purchased the sunflowers right away. In my heart, I knew I had to take them to the I Can Do It event. At the conference center, I asked the organizer to have them put on the stage with me.

When I walked onto the stage, I launched into my usual introductory lecture, explaining what mediumship is and what everyone in the audience could expect. All the while, I was aware of the mass of yellow sunflowers on the table beside me. I had barely finished my lecture when I felt the presence of those on the Other-Side draw close. Today, they were lining up as though waiting for the doors to open for Black Friday sales! It was going to be a busy afternoon.

Time was of the essence, so I didn't hesitate to let the spirits take over. The messages came thick and fast for moms, dads, children, husbands, wives, and friends. It was a beautiful and touching time.

As I felt the afternoon drawing to a close, I looked over at the sunflowers one more time. I could feel whoever urged me to buy the flowers finally making his presence known. It was as though he'd waited for everyone else to go first so he could get my undivided attention.

Now, I should point out that when I have a sign like this, I don't just blurt out, "Who here likes sunflowers?" If I did that, there would be a sea of hands shooting up! I need to trust that whatever message I'm supposed to deliver will come through with enough information from the spirit to make sure it's delivered to their loved one in a way that it could only be for them.

I could feel the excited energy of a young boy. He desperately wanted to talk to his mom. She'd been grieving for a long time because his death had been so sudden, she'd never been able to say good-bye. I quickly ascertained that he'd been her only child. I knew all too well the raw pain a mother feels when losing a child so young.

As the boy was linking with me, he made sure to give me enough evidence to single her out of an audience of over 1,000 people. He related clear information about his passing, including where and when it happened. He let me know what his mom was doing now and shared that she was never really sure about her belief in an afterlife. Finally, I heard as clear as day, in his very gentle and loving voice, "Please give her the sunflowers now."

Ah, so it was you who got me to buy them. Nice job, kid! I said to him in my mind.

"Mom, before we go, your son wanted to make sure that you knew it was really him and that he is okay. That there is an after-life, and you will see him again," I told her. From where the woman was sitting, she couldn't see the flowers on the table behind me. I turned around, picked them up, then walked over and placed the bouquet in her arms. "Your son wanted to give you these sunflow-ers! Apparently, they mean something to the both of you."

The woman took the flowers into both arms with a big smile and tears of joy. As she slowly turned toward the audience, she told them that sunflowers were her favorite flower. Her son would always give them to her on special occasions when he wanted to say, "I love you, mom!" It was never roses or daisies or any other flower — always sunflowers! She said they were special not just because of their beauty and radiance but also the fact they were from her son. They would joke that they were really "son-flowers." She went on to say that she still brings sunflowers to her son's grave. I ended the demonstration by giving her a hug and telling her, "He loves you, and it was his turn one more time to bring you *son-flowers!*"

Believing in the afterlife is not something that I or anyone else can force. You must start by opening up your heart and mind, and then the door can be opened to the Other-Side. Neither distance nor time, nor even death can ever separate you from your loved ones who have passed on — for love is truly everlasting.

JUST A THOUGHT AWAY

Here's a scenario that everyone will be familiar with. You think of someone out of the blue, so you pick up the phone and dial their number. The person who answers sounds somewhat surprised to hear your voice, saying, "I was just thinking about you!"

You might know a couple who often finishes each other's sentences or speaks the same words at the same exact time, whether it's between spouses, long-time partners, a parent and child, siblings, or close friends. We often laugh and shrug it off when this happens, putting it down to pure coincidence — but is it? How can we explain how family members often know when something's wrong with one another? Or why is it that certain people simply think of someone they haven't seen in a long time and then run into them later that day?

I don't believe these are coincidences or random bits of luck. These are what I refer to as "soul-to-soul connections." Many people consider it a form of telepathy, which is the ability to send and receive messages and information through the mind. *Telepathy* comes from the Greek root words *tele* and *pathy*, meaning "far feeling." It's a form of thought transference, where an exchange of energy acts as a communication link without using the physical senses. This is the same process used by those on the Other-Side when they want to communicate with us here in this physical dimension. The *energy* of thought is a spiritual power — and I believe it's the power of love that fuels this ability.

The power of love and thought is the force that continues to keep us connected to each other. How many times have you found yourself thinking about someone who's passed on? It's as though they just popped into your consciousness. It could be that, at that exact moment, they were lovingly thinking of you. Your loved ones are *really* just a thought away.

To illustrate this point, I'd like to share with you this lovely story of a child's belief in the power of thought. A little girl named Daisy passed to Spirit at the young age of 10. During her last days, Daisy looked up at her mother and told her that she was communicating with her little brother who had passed years earlier. In fact, she said, the little boy was standing right beside her, and the two were having quite a lively conversation.

"How do you speak to your little brother? I don't hear anything or see you moving your lips," asked the bewildered mother.

The grinning little girl answered, "Mommy, we just talk with our think."

Every time I hold a demonstration or give a private reading, I'm moved by the love from Spirit for those still here on earth. Remember, when you pass, your soul consciousness retains all your experiences and memories from this life. The entire history of your soul that's built up during your lifetime goes with you, as does the love for your friends and family. Those who are left behind often feel the caring emotion being sent from their spirit loved ones as it touches their hearts and souls.

Naturally, the link works both ways. You can send your thoughts and love to your people in the Spirit World.

ARE YOU REALLY THERE?

When someone passes and leaves this world, the usual familiar ways we use to communicate gets interrupted for a time until a new form of communication is established. That new form of communication happens through the mind.

With mediums who work mentally, the spirit of a loved one will link with the medium in a mind-to-mind telepathic connection. Once the link is established, the medium will receive information clairvoyantly, clairsentiently, or clairaudiently. The words, images, or feelings that are given from the spirit to the medium are all part of the authentication process of validating their identity.

However, you don't have to see a medium to communicate or feel close with a departed loved one. Many people who come to see me are longing to connect with the Other-Side, but in reality, they'll be receiving the information secondhand. Whether you lost someone recently or long ago, know that it's possible to connect with them yourself. They *do* receive your thoughts and do what they can to help.

Many people feel that their loved ones immediately become all knowing after they've passed. Although there's a natural progression of the soul, which I wrote about earlier, on the Other-Side, they're still the person you knew. They're learning new things themselves as they reacquaint themselves with their real home, the Spirit World. They do what they can to guide us; maybe nudge us in the right direction to be in the right place at the right time; and, of course, continue to love us. However, they cannot take away the karmic lessons that we are meant to learn here.

Your loved ones know what you're going through, and they realize how much you're missing them. Many people have said after a loss, "It's so strange, I feel as if they are right here with me." The reason for this is simple: they could possibly be there in spirit right next to you! While they try to comfort you, it's easy to miss those subtle signs they're sending you, especially during times of grief when your emotions are so sensitive.

When the time feels right, I recommend sitting in a comfortable place and trying to clear or calm down the chatter in your mind for a few moments. Now just focus on sending your thoughts to your loved ones. Send them your prayers, your wishes, your love . . . And, if need be, send your forgiveness.

Don't expect a dramatic response, like a scene from a movie where a spirit manifests right in front of you. You may not get a loud voice booming in your ear. You might even feel as though you're not having any success at first. However, please keep talking and sending those loving thoughts out. You'll know if you connect. It might be the most imperceptible feeling, as if a light flickered over your soul. You might get answers in ways you weren't expecting, so acknowledge them by letting them know you feel them.

Try to not let anyone talk you into believing it's just your imagination. You'll know in your heart when you have forged a loving link with your loved one. It's a totally different feeling than our own normal conscious thoughts! You'll understand what I mean when you experience it for the first time. Trust me when I say, "They want to talk to you — as much as you want to talk to them!"

Chapter 4

BUILDING THE BRIDGE

Death is, without a doubt, hardest on the living. Most people come to see me with a heavy heart following the loss of a loved one. They long for one last conversation, one last kiss, or that one final embrace to carry them through the rest of their lives here without their beloved. To them, I often ask the simple question: "Are you really without them?"

With the help of the Spirit People, I try my best to help others find comfort through the knowledge that there actually is an afterlife. Along with validating the existence of the Spirit World, I like to provide some basic tools and techniques so they can become more aware of the signs they might receive from their spirit loved ones in the future and hopefully even communicate with them independently.

Remember that whether one is incarnate (a spirit in a physical body) or discarnate (on the Other-Side as a spirit), you're still made up of the same spiritual source or energy as each other — you're connected, spirit to spirit. When you can have your own inner communion with someone who's passed, it provides firsthand evidence of the existence of the afterlife. It's the sort of confirmation that cannot be disputed or reasoned away. Once you learn to raise your own consciousness and have your own special connection with your loved ones on a spiritual level, then lasting proof and a loving communion is found.

When reaching out to those in the Spirit World, we have to do our part in building the bridge between this world and the next. The first step is raising your consciousness (also known as your energy, or vibration) so that as those on the Other-Side lower theirs, you'll be able to meet halfway, thereby bridging two realms.

There are several practices to help in raising one's consciousness using meditation as well as understanding and working with the chakras (energy centers), which I discuss in Part II of this book. I also encourage the use of your imagination. The power of your own imagination can take you to the higher planes where your loved ones in Spirit dwell. Imagination is the playground of your intuition, and it plays a vital role in your spiritual awareness. It can help you develop your psychic abilities, which have an important function in spirit communication.

Some years ago, I developed a special guided meditation called *The Bridge* (available for download through Hay House and johnholland.com). Using the power of music, color, and imagination, it creates a quiet space in your mind to meet your loved ones on the Other-Side. In the meditation, I have the listener climb a set of stairs. At the top of each stairway is a colored door, with each one representing a different chakra. Each door takes you higher and higher, which is all part of the gradual process of raising your consciousness. After you've climbed all the stairs and opened all the doors, you then enter a beautiful meadow. Using your imagination, you can feel, hear, see, and even smell all that is around you. Finally, you cross a small bridge and find yourself in a private gazebo, where a loved one joins you.

I've received many messages from people who have used the meditation, saying they had visits from parents, spouses, children, friends, and even beloved pets! You might now be asking: "But is it real?" or "Isn't it their imagination?" However, imagination is a creative power that God has imprinted on every soul. The process of stilling the mind through meditation, combined with the incredible power of your imagination, builds the etheric bridge of love that will keep you connected to your loved ones.

Although you might hope to connect with a specific loved one through meditation, you can't control who comes through. There's often a large crowd of spirits that stand behind humanity to serve and help, albeit unknown to most of those whom they seek to help. Sometimes, you might meet someone from your distant past, such as a teacher or even a guide. You may not always get whom you want; you'll get whom you need.

Next time you find yourself missing a loved one, try not to think they're in some faraway place. In reality, they're with you. They're not here in a physical body, but they're with you spiritually. Just remember that in the spiritual consciousness, there's absolutely no separation at all. To illustrate this point, I share the following story from a family that I am very close to. It shows that your loved ones are with you through all the bad times, as well as the good times!

The Bridge of Love

The bond that links us to our family is not just one of blood — but also of love. Chris and his wife, Claire, stood on the balcony in the Great Hall Meeting Room of Faneuil Hall in Boston. As beautiful as the historic building is, they weren't there to sightsee but to proudly watch their son, Charlie, be sworn in as an attorney.

The students' names were called one by one, and it was soon time for Charlie to stand up and accept his law degree. Just as Charlie's name was read, Chris began to feel a presence at his side. It felt as if his mom, who'd passed away years earlier, was standing right beside him. Chris shivered as it dawned on him what was happening. It hadn't been something he'd wished for or expected to happen, but he felt in his heart that she was there in spirit to support him and her grandson with her love. Never wanting to miss out on anything when she was alive, she clearly wanted to be part of her grandson's graduation!

As Chris's eyes welled up with tears, he felt another presence draw close and felt a hand on his shoulder. In his mind, he heard the voice of his dad, who'd passed years earlier, "Son, I'm so proud."

When Claire glanced up at her husband, she could clearly see that he was quite emotional, but thought it was because of their son graduating. Chris was proudly beaming from ear to ear with pride for his boy, but he was also overwhelmed by the love he was getting from his parents, who clearly wanted to be there, too!

Chris will never forget the look in his son's eyes as he smiled up at him and the rest of the family, and the tremendous feeling of love that surrounded him on that special day. There was no need for a spiritual medium that day! The love felt by him and his family had supplied all that was needed to create a bridge for his parents to step across. It left an impression on his heart that no one can ever take away from him.

THE POWER OF LOVE

Love is the foundation of our existence. Love is *not* just a feeling; it's also energy. Quantum physicists now confirm what mystics, gurus, and prophets have been telling us for over millennia: there's no such thing as solid matter. Everything in the Universe, including you and your thoughts, are made up of energy. The energy that makes up the stars in the sky — the energy that's coursing through the Universe — is the same energy within each and every one of us.

Since we are energy, we tune into and attract the same frequency that we resonate. This is the basis for the Law of Attraction. At its simplest definition, it's the belief that thoughts are magnets. You've probably heard the saying, Like attracts like. Well, it's really more about frequency attracting the same frequency. Positive thoughts will help you tune into your desired positive frequency.

If you send out loving thoughts, you'll attract compassion.
If you're afraid, you'll draw fear to yourself.
If you're kind, you'll attract kindness.
If you're grateful, you'll generate prosperity.

As you think, you begin to feel; as you feel, you vibrate; and as you vibrate, you start to attract . . . In other words, you attract exactly what you're resonating.

I believe that the energy of love is the most powerful and healing force that exists throughout the Universe. When you send out a loving thought to those in the Spirit World, they feel that love. It pulls them close to you and vice versa.

Your loved ones are constantly trying to get your attention and do whatever they can to let you know they're with you. However, during times of acute sadness and loneliness, it's not always possible to sense them or feel how much love you're being sent. The special bond of love you share with your loved ones, whether they're here or on the Other-Side, can never be broken.

WHY MAKE CONTACT?

People have many different reasons for wanting to communicate with Spirit or a specific loved one who has passed. Most of the time, we might think that we're the ones reaching out to make contact with the Other-Side, but in many cases, it's actually the Spirit World that initiates the communication. You may ask why would those on the Other-Side need to hear from *us*? Sometimes, the answer isn't profound but incredibly simple. As a medium, I've done countless readings in which I linked with a loved one who just wants to express their love, offer comfort, or come through with an apology for something they did while they were in the physical world.

Not too long ago, I did one of my small group readings that usually consist of 8 to 10 people. Even before the group arrives, I've prepared and have opened myself up to let the Spirit People who want to communicate come through. Some people attend these small groups longing to hear from a certain person with a message. But, sometimes, someone will come through whom they weren't expecting — sometimes it's even someone they didn't want to hear from! I can't control it because I'm not in charge; the Spirit World is. Mediumship cannot be forced, and I certainly can't call the dead. There's always a reason a certain spirit will come through.

I began this particular evening in my usual way, with my explanation of how I work and how spirits communicate using my psychic senses, enabling me to feel, hear, and see information. As part of my introduction, I explain that all I require from them is validation when they hear something correct or that they resonate with, but they should not *offer* any information. The less information the sitter gives me, the better. This night, as the eight people of the group sat in a circle, I could see anticipation in some eyes and sadness in others.

When I explain how I work, it's my way of beginning to open up and tune into the Spirit World. I send out my own private thoughts to the Spirit World, with a little greeting: *Hello, friends. Welcome. It's time to draw close to me.* As I'm talking, I'll usually feel them draw close to offer specific information about who they are and how they passed so that someone in the group can then validate the link and take the message.

On this particular night, I could feel a woman from the Other-Side who'd passed in her elderly years. The link was crystal clear, and she directed me to a woman named Ann. I turned to Ann and said, "I feel like I want to come to you. Do you understand an elderly woman named Helen who passed from a heart ailment and who is family?"

The look of disappointment on Ann's face surprised me. She said, "Yes, I know who she is. What does *she* want?" Obviously, she didn't care to hear from this woman! Ann went on to say that Helen was her mother-in-law, who'd passed away a couple of years ago. It became clear that while Helen was alive, she had never accepted Ann as her daughter-in-law. It was not an easy relationship for Ann, and she'd only put up with her mother-in-law for the sake of her husband.

I told Ann how much work it takes for the Spirit People to come through; if she allowed me, I was sure I could find out why Helen was coming through for her. Helen admitted that she'd treated Ann badly while she was alive, so there was no love lost between them. In fact, this evening, she had come through to ask for Ann's forgiveness. She acknowledged that she had been difficult not just to Ann, but to many other people in her life. I could feel the sincerity of her remorse, and I knew in my heart that it was important for Ann to hear this message.

Ann started to cry as she listened and nodded in agreement. She wondered what brought about the change of heart. I told her that when we pass, we go through a life review in which we get to experience the effects of our behavior, both positive as well as negative, on others while we were here on earth.

The act of forgiveness is incredibly powerful. It has the capacity to heal and transform. Forgiveness is all about choice. It doesn't necessarily mean releasing people from the responsibility for their actions; it's a matter of releasing the anguish that *your* soul is carrying around with it. When someone who passes asks for forgiveness and it's freely given, it helps them progress on the Other-Side in the same way it would here in the Physical Plane. Even if someone has passed and you never got the chance to say sorry to them, they know you're asking and they don't hold grudges.

After Helen passed on a few more pieces of evidence to Ann about her family, she said she hoped she could still be part of their lives. She ended her message with: "Please, I know you didn't come here hoping to hear from me, but I wanted to make up for how I treated you. Please accept my apologies as I hold open the door for your father to come through now." Ann put her hand on heart as she wiped her tears. As I felt Helen slowly step back, I hoped that Ann could find the space to forgive her mother-in-law.

As Ann's dad stepped forward, she began to smile. After all, it was her dad she was truly hoping to hear from. However, I don't believe it would have happened had Helen not come through first to build the bridge.

I've often said: "You may not always get whom you want — you get whom you need." But in this case, Ann received both the love from her mother-in-law, the love Helen could never show in this life, as well as the reunion with her dad whom she so missed.

I believe that Ann left a different woman that evening and, hopefully, with a little less weight on her soul.

AFTER-DEATH COMMUNICATIONS

There's a special language that transcends time and space — a language that's not constrained by the limitations of just words, but instead consists of signs, symbols, energy, and thoughts. This language can be heard and seen only when you truly pay attention . . . It's the language of Spirit.

Once a loved one passes and has settled again, they often do everything in their power to get your attention. When they send a sign, they're trying to tell us that they've survived death, that they love us, that they want us to live our lives to the fullest. Be watchful and pay attention, as it could be they who sent you that rainbow; that familiar song you heard on the radio; that special dream in which they appeared happy, healthy, and strong. Equally, it may be one of nature's beautiful creatures they so loved that suddenly appears, or the wonderful aroma of their favorite flower, or even a gentle touch on your face that you thought was just a breeze. They want you to know, "I love you, I am not gone, I am here right beside you. You may not see me, but I am here."

These special signs are what are known as after-death communications (ADCs). I also like to refer to them as "calling cards." (I wrote about these special signs and symbols in my last book, *The Spirit Whisperer*, but I feel it's very important to summarize again, since many people may not have read it.)

ADCs were brought to my attention by *Hello from Heaven!*, a book written by Judy and Bill Guggenheim. Judy and Bill did extensive research into after-death communication, interviewing more than 3,000 people who believed they'd been contacted by a deceased loved one. The book includes over 300 stories of ADCs, and Judy and Bill's research powerfully concludes that an estimated 60 to 120 *million* Americans have experienced some form of an ADC. That amazing number of people tells us that ADCs are quite normal and happen all the time.

Many of us have experienced synchronistic events or received signs and symbols from those on the Other-Side. It's easy, however, to miss them or conveniently explain them away as "coincidences." In fact, I recently received a sign that I came close to explaining away — even though I've been doing this work for many years!

I was walking past my kitchen counter one night, thinking of my mom who had passed a few years before. Suddenly I heard a *clink*. I noticed that the pens and pencils I had in a cup on the counter somehow all shifted to the other side of the cup. Earlier the pens and pencils were on the right of the cup, and now all of them lay to the left. I remember thinking to myself, *Mmm, it must have created a breeze when I was walking by.* Yeah, right! How fast would I have had to have been walking to create that type of wind current? I thought about it and realized there is no way those pens could have moved on their own. With a big smile on my face, I said, "Thanks, Mom! I get the message!"

It's important to stress here that ADCs are *not* facilitated through a psychic or a medium. You don't need some sort of tool to receive or interpret them. These are spiritual experiences that happen spontaneously. They come in many forms and are usually quite personal. Some people have special signs that are unique to them. Here's one touching story of undying love that I heard recently that reinforces this point.

Sand Dollars: Tokens of Love

They say that the sea speaks to the soul, and many times its sandy beaches hold very special treasures. Jeri and David had this beautifully romantic ritual that they always did together. They would head off to the local beach, not to watch the sunsets but to stroll, holding hands as they watched the beautiful ocean waves roll in. One thing they would usually do whenever they were on this specific beach was to look for sand dollars that had washed ashore. It was their special time together, and it would be rare for them not to bring a few sand dollars home. Every token became a special memory of their romantic walks together. Little did they know that one of these cherished treasures would someday mean more than they could ever have imagined.

They married and had a daughter, Riley, and two boys, Tegan and Logan. Everything seemed almost perfect. It came as a terrible shock when David developed an aggressive cancer and passed away far too quickly. Jeri lost the love of her life and her best friend; their children lost a doting father.

One day, some months after David passed, Jeri was hanging out in the living room with her youngest son, Logan, who was 14 years old at the time. They'd both been thinking about David a lot recently. Logan was starting a new school year, his first year in high school, and she knew that he wished his dad could be there for support on this big day. Sensing Logan's mood, Jeri reached out and whispered, "Do you want to join me for a walk down on Sand Dollar Beach?" Before she'd even finished asking, Logan had hopped off the couch with a smile and run to the door. That was his answer!

It was the first week in September, and the beach was practically deserted. Without a word, they both started looking for sand dollars, just as Jeri and David had done together so many times before. They walked up and down the beach, pushing mounds of sand aside, scouring the shore for their treasure. Yet no matter how hard they looked, they couldn't find a single sand dollar. Logan's face couldn't hide his frustration and disappointment. Jeri looked up to the sky and said in her mind, *David, please send us a sign. Logan is starting school tomorrow, and he really could use a hello from Heaven from you right now.*

Jeri turned away for a moment, so Logan wouldn't see the tear trickling down her face. It was then that she noticed a small boat approaching the shore. She could have sworn it wasn't there before, and she didn't know where it had come from. The man in the boat stood up waving and yelling, "Hi! Are you looking for sand dollars?"

"*Yes!*" the two yelled back in unison, a resounding roar of excitement.

The man smiled and pointed, "Give that sand bar over there a try!"

Jeri and Logan thanked the man and ran across the beach. She glanced back for a second, but he'd already turned the boat around and left. She thought how strange it was that this man hadn't asked them if they were looking for shells, sea glass, or even heart rocks. Instead, he'd specifically mentioned sand dollars!

Logan ran ahead excitedly, hoping to find just one memento. He soon saw, to his amazement and delight, a crisp sand dollar sticking out of the sand! Then another and then another lay before him. The more they looked, the more they found.

Jeri smiled as she heard her son shouting in joy, "Mom, Mom, here's another one!" They found so many, they filled every pocket they had. As they walked back up the shore, they counted a total of 43 sand dollars. Logan looked up at her, smiling, his eyes full of tears. "Mom, this is better than winning the lottery!"

In her heart, Jeri knew it had been David who'd helped them. She closed her eyes as she felt a gentle breeze caress her face like a kiss. Her skin tingled with his presence.

Logan kept asking, "Mom, how did the guy in the boat know what we were looking for? I bet it was Dad saying hi!"

I'm sure there will be many more sand dollars (and other ADCs) waiting for Jeri and her family. They will always bring back happy memories of the sun, the laughs, the carefree walks, the gentle embraces, and the loving kisses that will be treasured always. Simple signs can be profound. A special symbol, unique to you, has a way of filling your heart. Now, whenever Jeri walks along that special beach, whether alone or with her children, she knows that David is right beside her.

ADCs THROUGH DREAMS

Over the years, I've heard thousands of stories of ADCs. One man's house filled with the smell of pipe tobacco, immediately triggering memories of his dad lighting up his pipe. A woman told me she felt a kiss on her forehead and knew it was from her husband who'd passed suddenly. Another told me of the indent in the blanket on her bed, which was the same size of a pet who had recently passed. While there are hundreds of ways spirits reach out through ADCs, the number one way is dreams.

When you're asleep, your mind is not working overtime. As it's calm and relaxed, your left brain (the analytical side) is able to take a much-needed break. This is the easiest time for spirits to sneak into your consciousness and psyche. It may not happen right away, however. It took my mom a year to visit my dreams after she'd passed. I didn't demand it, but somehow I knew it would happen eventually.

I love asking audiences, "Who's had a dream of a loved one, when you knew for a fact that it really was them?" Immediately, a sea of hands will go up. Whether the dream happened days ago, weeks ago, or even years ago, the memory of that special ADC is usually as fresh for the person as though it were dreamed last night.

When I ask people to describe what happened in the dream, what was said, and how the person looked, the answers are usually always the same. First, their loved ones always appear healthy and vibrant, even if there was illness, age ravaged their bodies, or they passed due to some trauma. They appear smiling, healthy, and perfect. Many people distinctly remember saying in their dreams, "What are you doing here — you're dead!"

The messages that come back in a dream are usually short. Without opening their mouths, spirits will use thought to convey that they live on, that they're alive, and that they still love you. Most important, they *want* you to go on with your lives here, to be happy, and to know that they'll see you again.

In these special dreams, you may just get a hug that feels so real, so loving, that when you wake up, you have tears in your eyes. Have faith and trust that it *really* was them who came to visit and held you close in that loving embrace.

Of course, not every dream you have of a loved one is a legitimate ADC. It may be your own mind working through your bereavement process, especially if the dream is disturbing or your loved one appears in a distressing or negative way. You'll know which ones are genuine ADCs because they'll have a sense of clarity to them, being more detailed, loving, enjoyable, and above all positive.

I recommend keeping a journal beside your bed to record your dreams, whether they're ADCs or not. This will get you in the habit of paying attention to and retaining details of your dreams. If you want to have an ADC dream of a loved one, then a good way to start is to spend some time in quiet reflection or meditation. Send a thought out to that person. Gather up all the love you have in your heart and think of them. Ask them to appear in your dream, and tell them that you're ready and willing to receive a message.

Remember, while you may just get that person, don't be surprised if you get a message from someone you least expect!

COMMON SIGNS OF ADCs

You might have already detected a spirit presence yourself at some point, even if you didn't totally realize it. For example, have you ever felt a loved one standing beside you, but you explained it away as wishful thinking or your imagination? Have you seen something out of the corner of your eye, but when you looked at it directly, it was gone? Have you ever heard your name being called and no one was there? These are all typical examples of some of the ways your loved ones will try to make their presence known to you.

Since there are so many ways that spirits can send you a sign, I'll list a few of some of the most popular:

- Feeling a loved one's presence
- Finding shiny coins, such as pennies and dimes
- Electrical items switching on and off
- Phones ringing and the name of the person who passed being displayed on the caller ID
- Nature signs, such as the appearance of rainbows
- Sudden appearances of specific animals, birds, and insects — butterflies are a big sign!
- Same set of numbers keeps showing up
- Scents coming from no known physical source
- Items going missing and then suddenly appearing out of nowhere
- A favorite song playing on the radio just as you think about someone
- Synchronistic events and other strange "coincidences"
- Seeing someone off in the distance who seems to be a duplicate of a loved one who has passed
- A loved one's name showing up just when you were thinking about them

These are just a few examples of the many different ways in which your loved ones may try to get your attention. Trust me, they'll try anything to reach out to you. Try not to *demand* a sign; it's more likely to come when you least expect it. Just as you have a life here, so do spirits on the Other-Side, so they may not always be at your beck and call.

No matter what ADC you receive, they're always meant to be loving, joyful, and positive. They are usually received exactly when you need it. They shouldn't be scary or frightening, or cause you more grief. Again, it's spirits' way of saying, "I love you, and I'm with you always."

If you believe in ADCs but have yet to experience one, know that spirits often take their cues from you. If they know that you're still emotional and an ADC may upset you or increase your sadness, they might pass a message through someone else until you're ready to receive one directly.

When you feel you're *open* and ready to *receive* a sign, put a loving thought out to them. Ask them to show you a sign, one that you'll know is from them. Keep an open mind, without a set expectation of what you *want* your sign to be. You may get the same symbol over and over, or you could get a different message every time. Trust me, they know when you're ready and how to get your attention. Be thankful for them, cherish them, and hold them close to your heart, for they truly are *hellos from Heaven.*

"I'M RIGHT BESIDE YOU": WAYS
OF MAKING YOUR OWN CONTACT

If spirits can reach out to you, then it's fair to say that you can reach out and communicate with them. Best of all, you don't need a medium to do it for you nor do you need special abilities to make this type of loving connection on your own. There are numerous ways to communicate with passed loved ones and stay in touch every day, but you have to start with a strong mind-set and a belief that it *is* possible!

I want to reiterate that when someone passes, they *don't* become all knowing. They may gently guide you and assist you whenever they can, but they can't interfere with the karmic lessons that you're meant to learn in your lifetime. I recall a lovely woman who came to see me a few years ago. She was happy with the reading, as her mom had come through loud and clear. However, as she was leaving, she said, "I was a little disappointed that my mom didn't tell me whether I should divorce my husband." I told her that is not her mother's job on the Other-Side to make such decisions for her. There are certain lessons that we need to go through here, and we cannot look to Spirit for all our decisions and answers we seek in this life.

The following techniques are just a few ways that you can connect with your loved ones *without* having mediumistic abilities. If you do want to go further with your psychic and mediumship abilities, then these techniques are a good start to developing them. (I will expand even further on mediumship development in Part II of this book.)

While there are many ways to communicate with Spirit, it's not a one-size-fits-all type of thing. What works for one person might not work for you. It's a matter of trying different techniques to find the one that works for you. Hopefully one of the following will suit both you and your loved ones to perfectly build that loving bridge across two realms.

Meditation: Into the Stillness

When communicating with the Other-Side, it's important to start by clearing your thoughts and stilling your mind. Meditation helps construct the bridge between two realms by raising your consciousness. By meditating, you're making room for Spirit People to imprint their thoughts on your mind.

Meditation is a state of being in which your active mind slows down; it's a time of quiet reflection to achieve clarity. With time and practice, meditation can take you to a place where you silence your mental chatter. In doing so, you become increasingly aware of the subtle and shifting energies within you. It may seem impossible, but you can actually train yourself to watch your thoughts come into your mind and go right out again, much like the ebb and flow of an ocean's tide. Soon the thoughts that would invade your mind when you first started to meditate will lose their power to influence your consciousness.

There are many ways to meditate, and you can choose whatever practice is most effective for you. I offer some valuable meditation techniques in one of my earlier books, *Psychic Navigator.*

Try meditating for 10 to 15 minutes at first. As you become more proficient, gradually extend the length of time for as long as you feel necessary or are comfortable with. It's important to dedicate time for meditating, as though you're making a date with yourself. I recommend that you try to meditate at the same time every day and, if possible, in the same place. By doing this, you're building up the energy in that space. Not only will you feel the calm energy in this place, but also your bridge will become stronger and stronger to the Other-Side when you meditate. Don't be surprised if people comment about the sense of tranquility and peacefulness when they step into your meditation area. It's all about energy.

Invite Them

Your loved ones know that you're reaching out to them, so invite them to your own private get-together by following these simple steps:

- Find a comfortable place, such as your meditation area, and safely light a small votive candle on a table. Place a picture of your loved one right in front of you. Try to find the happiest picture you have of them because, in reality, that's how they look now! Look into their eyes in the picture for a few moments. See the light that's coming from them and remember that beautiful image in your mind.

- Now, set an intention that you're open to receiving messages or signs from your chosen loved one. By setting the intention, you're lovingly inviting them with an open heart and mind. You are safe and always in control because you're the one who's reaching out to your loved one. If you feel the need for some protection, surround yourself with white light and ask to receive only what is for your highest good.

- Close your eyes and meditate to clear your mind to make room for them. Hold the image of your loved one from the picture in your mind's eye.

- Send out a loving thought and invite them to join you. Let them know it's okay to come to you now. Remember they take their cues from you when connecting and will only connect when they know it's not going to upset you.

- Ask a question in your mind and be patient. Try not to have any expectations. Patience is key here in making sure you're receiving a message that didn't come from your own imagination. You may feel your loved one draw close to you, or you might feel a breeze, a light kiss, or a gentle embrace. You may hear a single word or a sentence, or you may see an image or a symbol. You may even notice a scent like a perfume or a flower. (Don't worry if you feel you didn't get a message or sign right away; you may get an answer when you least expect it.)

- Most important, trust what you're getting and don't try to manipulate it or make it fit some preconceived idea of what you wanted or needed to hear. As I've said previously, they no longer have a physical body, so they're also learning and need to establish this new form of communication. If it's the first time, then it's a learning experience for both of you. Since you're both learning to communicate with each other, initially it's totally fine to just chat, without expecting anything more or an answer to your question. Each time you talk to them in your mind, the stronger your link will become. The more you do this, the more proficient you'll get in building the bridge to your loved one.

- Always end by thanking your loved one for coming. Say, "See you later" rather than "Good-bye," as you know you can connect with them whenever you wish.

Building a Psychic Database

Spirit speaks to me in words, images, feelings, and symbols. I remember a simple yet profound saying I learned when I was studying mediumship: Spirit never wastes a thought.

When a spirit sends me a symbol, it's all about association. For example, when I get a maple leaf in a message, it often means there's a connection to Canada. Spirit knows that to me, a maple leaf represents the country rather than the word *maple*, so when I receive this symbol I don't go off on a tangent. A waterfall always signifies upstate New York, a rainbow shows me an artist. When a birthday cake is put in front of me, it means a birthday is happening now. If a spirit impresses upon me the image of the number one, it means the person who I'm doing the reading for is their only child or the firstborn, or they took care of them before they died. A pair of scissors always means that someone here or over there is a hair stylist. These are just a few examples of images that frequently come to me.

When I first began to connect with Spirit, I would write down in my journal all the symbols and images I'd receive. I'd ask myself, "What does this symbol mean to me," or "What does this mean to [the mom, dad, child, etc.] who has passed that I'm connecting with?" The more you ask this type of question, the more you'll notice the same symbols coming to you for similar situations.

Over the years, this has helped me build up a "psychic database," as I like to call it, filled with all these memories, images, symbols, and signs. It's important to note, however, that these are *my* symbols. A symbol or image may have a strong meaning to me, while the same image can have a totally different meaning for someone else. That's why, when you receive messages from Spirit, it's important to start building up your *own* database of symbols. In your journal, detail your analysis and interpretation of the symbols you receive as you're trying to connect with your loved ones. Create a language that's personal to *you*, and soon the Spirit People will begin to use whatever they can that's in your database to get their message across. It really is the ultimate partnership!

Personal Items

Everything contains energy that vibrates at its own unique frequency; this includes objects and personal items. When a friend of mine wants to talk to her husband who passed away a year ago, she plays with his wedding ring that she now wears on a chain around her neck. It's as though it's her unique way of calling him. When Rose, a client of mine, wants to connect to her grandmother, she reaches up and touches the antique brooch that she gave her. One man told me that he reaches for his dad's sweatshirt every time he wants to feel close to him.

Most of us have personal items that belonged to someone else or that were gifted or passed down to us from someone special. We treasure these items that belonged to our loved ones. When trying to connect to Spirit, hold your special item and send out a loving thought to them. What this is really doing is sending out an invitation to let them know you're thinking of them. If you find yourself suddenly picking up, playing with, or touching your special object, it could be because they're thinking of you right then. This is their way of reaching out to you.

Say Prayers

I know many of you who are reading this book are aware that we're part of something far greater than ourselves. Some people call it *God*, *Spirit*, or *Creator*, just to name a few terms. Most religions agree that there's one true Source that cares about you, no matter who you are or what your personal circumstances. It makes sense that we naturally yearn to connect with this Divine Source. It wants to respond to you and your needs, but it wants you to respond back. It wants to help you, but there has to be two-way communication.

Prayers (whether spoken or unspoken) are how we ultimately communicate with God, a higher power, the Universe, or what I refer to as the Divine Source. Simply put, when you pray, you connect. It's a way for us as human beings to develop a relationship with Source. This connection can benefit our lives on so many levels. We can pray to and for our loved ones, and they also can pray for us. It works both ways. I also find it helpful to pray *to* certain loved ones. I believe that prayers are, in fact, thoughts infused with love.

Even if you don't fully believe in a supreme deity or follow a certain faith, there may be times when you find yourself offering a small prayer of gratitude, whether or not you're totally aware of whom you're thanking. Praying enables you to forge a relationship with something or someone that you may not be able to see but is truly there. Preacher Max Lucado beautifully described the power of prayer: "Our prayers may be awkward. Our attempts may be feeble. But since the power of prayer is in the one who hears it and not in the one who says it, our prayers do make a difference."

Mirror Gazing: A Visionary Experience

Can we really see our departed loved ones right in front of us? According to Dr. Raymond Moody, this is possible through *mirror gazing*, which is also known as *scrying*. He developed his own mirror-gazing technique using his Psychomanteum Chamber, which was inspired by the ancient techniques used 2,500 years ago at the Oracle of the Dead in Ephyra, Greece. Over the years, I've heard him speak many times of the people who have gazed into the mirror in his Psychomanteum Chamber and subsequently had their own personal contact with their departed loved ones.

You don't need to have your own chamber; a simple mirror can provide the necessary gateway. Simply follow these steps.

- Sit comfortably and look into the depth of a clear mirror. I recommend that you have either a tall mirror in front of you or one on a table, so you can easily gaze into it.

- Place a candle behind you and away from your gaze. You want to gently illuminate the room with soft light, just bright enough to see your reflection in the mirror. I've found that the lower the lighting is in the room, the better the results.

- Deeply relax your body until it feels heavy. When you're ready, try not to really see anything or strain your eyes as you gaze into the mirror. Relax your eyes and just gaze gently. Some people have said they noticed the mirror becoming cloudy or a fine gray mist appearing. If you experience this, it's quite normal; it's not your eyes playing tricks on you. Let it happen, because this is usually a sign that a vision is about to appear.

- When you begin to see images, please don't try to control them. Let them flow naturally as you remain relaxed. You may see a loved one, a pet, or even a special memory from your past. Some people have reported that images took on a 3-D effect, so that they were seeing things outside the mirror. Images may last seconds or even minutes. The more you practice this, the more proficient you will become and the longer the visions will last. However, don't be surprised or worried if you don't see anything initially; you might feel, rather than see, your loved ones around you.

- I recommend that you write down your experiences in as much detail as possible. There may come a time when you need to reflect on an image that appeared to you or you might need some inspiration to give you a loving lift.

Electronic Voice Phenomenon (EVP)

It's widely speculated that Thomas Edison was working on a machine just before he died that would enable people to talk to the dead. It's been dubbed the "spirit phone," and if anyone were to have invented an ingenious piece of equipment like this, surely it would have been Edison. Of course, the device was never found, but there could be another way to speak to people on the Other-Side electronically!

Within the field of parapsychology, extensive research is being carried out on the subject of electronic voice phenomenon (EVP). EVPs are sounds that are recorded electronically that are not audible to the human ear. Parapsychologist Konstantins Raudive popularized the idea in the 1970s. He described an EVP as typically brief, usually the length of a word or short phrase. I've heard these EVPs, and although they're often accompanied by static, a clear voice can be heard within.

This technique may not be for everyone, but some people are having success with it when it comes to connecting to the Other-Side. If you're intrigued and wish to look into EVP, then I remind you to stay grounded and trust your intuition anytime you're being introduced to something that's outside of your own sphere of understanding. If it doesn't feel right, then don't pursue it.

Communications Induced by Therapist

I love how Spirit and synchronicity work together bringing in or manifesting exactly what you need! I was looking to add just one more technique on how you can make your own contact with your loved ones, and of course, "they" didn't let me down. During the research that I undertook to write this particular section of the book, a nice gentleman reached out to give me information about his organization. His name was R. Craig Hogan, Ph.D., and he's the president of the Afterlife Research & Education Institute. I told him he contacted me at *just* the right time.

Craig and a team of founders have devoted themselves to educating people on the different methods of afterlife communication, so that every person can communicate with their passed loved ones. They're dedicated to sharing their knowledge about the research on the advancements in communications technology and altered states of the human mind. They've highlighted some of the most effective methods of afterlife communication not available until today. He claims, "We're witnessing the dawning of the day when afterlife communication will be commonplace."

I found it most synchronistic that he reached out just as I was writing this section on how people can connect to their passed loved ones without a medium. I enjoyed our conversation so much that I had him on my weekly Hay House Radio show, *Spirit Connections*. During the interview, he told me of a new and fascinating technique called "repair and reattachment grief therapy" that's getting a good response from the people who took part in a study with trained licensed therapists.

This procedure is administered by state-licensed mental health therapists, marriage and family counselors, social workers, psychologists, and psychiatrists. It can reduce or virtually eliminate a person's deep grief. One's interpretation of the death of a loved one, including the negative beliefs, images, feelings of guilt and anger, and trauma, are reoriented and replaced by reassurance, joy, renewed feelings of love and connection, and peace. The sadness at the separation through death is usually desensitized so the person doesn't remember it in the same way and the sadness eventually dissipates. People don't forget their loved ones, but after a repair and reattachment grief therapy session, they see them in a better light, and most of the time the sadness has gone.

The method itself does not induce the connections. Instead, experiencers are opening their own connections with their loved ones in the afterlife, while being *guided* by a licensed psychotherapist. The psychotherapist is not a medium and has no influence over the nature or content of the connection. The afterlife connections occur naturally and effortlessly between the experiencers and their loved ones, emerging when the experiencers enter a receptive mode, just as sleep follows naturally from relaxing into a comfortable bed. The sessions normally last four to five hours, during which the person usually has an ADC.

Now, you might be wondering; *Is this a real connection or is it happening in the mind of the experiencer? Is this just wishful thinking or imagination?* Suffice it to say that the people who went through this procedure are benefitting and feel that these were real experiences with their loved ones.

As I've stated, this is a new technique. As people are being helped with their grief and having encounters with the Spirit World, I'm sure we'll be hearing more about it in the future. If you're interested in this procedure, it's *very* important to seek out therapists who have been properly trained, so in the reference section at the back of this book, you'll find information on the Afterlife Research & Education Institute.

It's quite natural and normal to want to explore the subject of life after life. Mankind has been doing it for thousands of years. I hope this brief overview has given you a few ideas and techniques that will help you to stay in touch and communicate with your loved ones. Most importantly, keep an open mind. Try different techniques until you find the one that works for you. Every time you connect with a loved one, it builds that bridge and makes the connection between the two realms stronger and stronger.

Of course, there are many emotions that surface when we lose someone we love, so take time to acknowledge and sit with those emotions. They do live on because we never *really* lose someone we care about. No matter what, we're still connected to them. Neither death nor time can ever rob you of that. Love never dies.

Chapter 5

MEDIUMS AND SEEKERS

Here in the 21st century, what with the hundreds of television channels and programs to choose from, I feel we've become a more aware and open-minded society. Through movies, books, and our social-media connections, people are more and more knowledgeable about mediums and our work. Technology has brought niche subjects such as mediumship into every home, and it's now accessible on almost any platform by anyone.

I'm thankful that reputable mediums are being introduced to the public, yet there are still many misconceptions of what a medium is and how mediumship functions. For example, when I began to work as a medium, I did private sittings from my home. On more than one occasion, I'd answer the door and people would immediately ask: "Is your father home?"

I'd ask, "Who are you looking for?"

"John Holland," they'd reply.

Smiling, I'd say, "Well, that would be me!"

I always found it humorous because people would apologize, laugh, or simply look embarrassed. They'd admit that I was not what they were expecting. I'm sure they were expecting an older gentleman rather than a young guy in jeans and a T-shirt! One time, before one of my shows, I remember walking from my car to the venue and overhearing two women who were looking at my photo on the brochure. I overheard one say, "You know, Helen, he looks so normal." I wanted to chime in and say, "I'm sorry, ladies, I left my cape and turban at the house!"

Too many people believe what they see on television or in movies, where mediums are all too often portrayed overdramatically. One such movie, *The Sixth Sense*, became a worldwide hit in 1999. It featured a troubled boy (Cole Sear) who was continually terrified by menacing spirits. If those on the Other-Side showed up to me in the forms they did in this movie, trust me: I wouldn't be working as a medium!

I'm sure you've seen portrayals of mediums sitting in a darkened room, spookily lit by candles. Their eyes roll back in their heads as they squirm in their chairs and talk in a trancelike state. All the while, eerie music plays in the background!

I understand it's all done for dramatic effect, but I want you to understand that real mediums look and dress just like you, and spirits don't walk around looking terrifying. I work hard to take all the spooky misconceptions out of mediumship. Why add an unnecessary layer of fear and anxiety to the whole process of death? For many, the fear of death is enough, without added drama.

Before we delve into the definition of a medium, how they work, and what you can expect, please let me first clear up one important and essential misconception that many people often believe . . .

THE DIFFERENCE BETWEEN PSYCHICS AND MEDIUMS

A psychic and a medium are *not* the same thing. There's a big difference between practicing as a psychic versus a medium. As the clever saying goes: all mediums are psychic, but not all psychics are mediums. Let me explain this more fully.

A psychic reads your aura to see your past, present, and potential future, whereas a medium gets their information directly from those on the Other-Side. When it comes to information, you could say that a psychic *perceives* whereas a medium *receives*.

Well-trained psychics are wonderful for assisting people with day-to-day issues, career decisions, and guidance. Often, they're confirming what the sitter's intuition is saying. Psychics can offer great support to navigate some of life's hurdles and avoid the pitfalls. Their role is to offer guidance through psychic advice.

Please note that, as always, you have free will. It's only advice, not instructions, that is being given. Use your own judgment to know whether it feels right to you. If you're interested in sitting with a psychic, please go to someone reputable or one who is referred by word of mouth. Walk away immediately if a psychic mentions a curse or your needing to make multiple payments to get out of bad luck!

I started off doing psychic readings in my early years, as I discovered I had the ability. Then the Other-Side started to show up, and I quickly realized that some people could be both a psychic and a medium. Nowadays, I'm sure to explain to the sitter the difference between information I'm getting psychically and what's coming through from their loved ones. A good psychic medium should always explain the difference in the source of the information that's coming through.

I appreciate that some people may be apprehensive when they come to see me, whether it's because they don't understand the process or they have preconceived ideas from what they've seen in the entertainment industry. I can assure you that nothing scary or dramatic happens when Spirit People come through and relay their messages. After all, they're still your friends and family. The same people you loved here will come through just as you remembered them, whether they were loving, humorous, astute, happy, or even grumpy! Trust me when I say that you'll be able to identify them. They go to great lengths to confirm their identity using personal information known only to them and the recipient to help validate who they are.

When someone sits with me, it's like sitting with a friend at a family gathering. There's often tears as the reunion commences but also plenty of laughter. Your loved ones want you to be happy! After all, we're the ones still here who need support to go on. I'm always thrilled when a reading goes well and the energy flow is strong and consistent for the spirit's personality or true essence to come through, especially if they have a sense of humor. I never know who's enjoying the sitting more . . . me, the spirit, or the sitter?

WHAT IS A MEDIUM?

Even though the physical world and the Spirit World are independent of each other, the two are in a constant interaction and, through mediumship, these two realms can consciously communicate with each other. A medium, in the simplest of terms, acts as the "middle man," forming the bridge that links this world and the next. A medium has highly tuned psychic senses and receives information mentally from the discarnate (Spirit Person) through his or her abilities of clairvoyance, clairaudience, or clairsentience. Once the link has been validated, information is then passed on to the sitter. It's the medium's job to relay what they're receiving without questioning it or putting their own connotations on it. If a question needs be asked by the medium, it should only be to validate the information or the evidence they're receiving. A good medium should never offer up vague, general information; it should be specific to you, your family, and the person that has passed.

As a medium and spiritual teacher, I feel it's my job to educate the people who seek me out for a private sitting as well as my audiences on the process of how mediumship works and what they can expect when I link with Spirit. I tell my audiences that we mediums don't call the dead — *they* call *us*! It's my belief that a medium can't call up a spirit on demand. The Spirit People are in control of when, where, and how they choose to communicate.

Remember, information is not coming *from* the medium, but *through* the medium. Every sitting is a three-way process, or conversation, as everyone is involved: the spirit, the medium, and the recipient.

We're all made of a spiritual force, so you might understand when I say that the information is coming *from* spirit (your loved ones) *through* spirit (the medium) *to* spirit (the sitter). We're all connected. Each part has to be in sync to make a strong connection and ensure a constant clear flow of information. It's not always easy! I mean, it's hard enough to get three people in one room to agree on what to have for dinner. That's why I highly recommend that everyone have an open mind when seeing a medium.

Albert Best, a famous Scottish medium, was once asked if demonstrations of mediumship really convince audiences. He answered, "We can't convince anybody of anything. We can only sow a seed. The greatest thing we can do is to stimulate people to find out more for themselves. We can't take away the pain of loss, but if we have taken away the fear of death, if we have given hope where there was none before, then we have done something worthwhile."

I feel that pretty much says it all.

HOW THE INFORMATION COMES THROUGH

It's not an easy job communicating with someone who no longer has a physical body, especially when communication is no longer done in spoken words. Images, sounds, and symbols come through the mind, and as a medium, we have to interpret them as best we can and with the information we're given.

For instance, at a public demonstration at a local bookstore, I felt a young man come through in my mind. He was sending me strong feelings about baseball and visuals that, even though they didn't mean much to me, included his beloved baseball bat. The link was so strong; it felt as if an invisible director were guiding me. I turned to a certain part of the bookstore and said, "Who here in this section understands a young man who passed away suddenly and might have been buried with a baseball bat?"

I noticed one woman had a perplexed look on her face. After a few seconds, she spoke up, "Does it have to be a baseball *bat*?"

I replied, "All I know is that their burial has something to do specifically with baseball."

Well, what she said next surprised the audience as well as myself. She said that her friends' son, whom she'd loved and adored, had passed away as a young man. He'd loved baseball so much that his dad had an urn specifically made in the shape of a baseball to hold his ashes. I heard a gasp around the bookstore as she told this story. It just proves that when spirits want to get a message through, they will do anything and everything they can!

In Chapter 4, I wrote about building a psychic database, through which Spirit will use everything that a medium has ever learned or experienced in their own life as a reference. Albert Best, whom I mentioned earlier, worked as a mailman for many years. When he worked as a medium, he'd often receive first names, last names, and addresses from the Other-Side. When John Edward does a demonstration as a medium, he often receives detailed medical conditions that confirm how the spirit passed as well as precise movie references sometimes. It's not surprising to discover that he once worked as a phlebotomist and worked in a video store when he was younger.

Since I'm half Italian, I'm good with Italian references. I also love art and often take drawing and art classes, so it makes sense that I often receive symbols and pictures, which enable me to quickly interpret the message and make sense of it. One single image for me can convey a whole story.

Because alcoholism has plagued my family for generations, I have enough associations to help me confirm when alcohol is involved in a message, whether it's a spirit's ultimate cause of death or a recurring theme during their lifetime. My brother is a nurse who has worked in several hospitals, so medical professions are something that I can relate to. If I knew all about plumbing,

I'm sure Spirit would find a way to use visual prompts of copper pipes, faucets, and more in delivering a message.

I encourage you to study whatever you feel drawn to: look at picture books, learn human anatomy, do whatever it takes to create a psychic database from which Spirit can draw. The more knowledge you have, the more Spirit has to work with to get their message across.

MEDIUMSHIP AND SPIRITUALISM

Communicating with the Spirit World and honoring our ancestors has been practiced since the beginning of civilization. Many cultures all over the world have their own unique ceremonies and their own definition of a medium, including the medicine man in Native American culture, the high priest in ancient Egypt, and the priestess of Delphi in Greece. In the 19th century, Spiritualism brought mediumship to the world's attention.

Many years ago, as I set out to study mediumship, I was introduced to the teachings of Spiritualism, which completely resonated with my own thinking and aspirations. This belief system has its foundations centered on the continuity of life and communication with Spirit through the spiritual ability of mediumship. For many, it's also a religion, a philosophy, and even a way of life.

The Spiritualist faith has a very calming and healing effect; it's their belief (which, of course, I share) that we don't die and our loved ones who've passed on are still very much alive and well in Spirit. Sadly, once again, too many Hollywood movies have portrayed this faith in a somewhat eerie light, giving the wrong impression about what it truly is.

Most religions have some belief in the afterlife. Although I value what Spiritualism teaches, I'm not trying to convert anyone. I try to encompass and honor many religions, such as Catholicism, Buddhism, Kabbalah, and more. I feel that each serves its own unique purpose in providing tools and teachings for our personal spiritual journey. I like to use the analogy of a wheel, with each spoke representing a different religion or faith. Although each is independent of the other, the wheel is going to the same destination.

We're all born with the spark from the Divine (our spirit), so when our spirit finally crosses over, that spark will leave the vessel it's encased in (our body), and slip back into the Spirit World where we originated. We all survive death no matter what religion, if any, we choose to believe.

Through philosophy and practical demonstrations, Spiritualism aims to provide evidence that a part of everyone (spirit), continues to exist after death and for eternity. Spiritualism does not tie its followers to a creed or dogma, but the philosophy is based on the seven principles that were written in the 19th century through the mediumship of Emma Hardinge Britten. They are widely accepted by Spiritualists and Spiritualist organizations around the world.

I have written about Spiritualism and my own experiences in Spiritualist Churches before, but I wanted to include this once again because I feel that if you, the reader is interested in mediumship or learning about the survival of the soul and the Spirit World, then it's worth repeating so you have a better understanding for yourself. Spiritualism provided me with the strict training and ethics I needed in my early life as an emerging medium. I was blessed to spend over two years studying in England and owe much to the Spiritualists, who guided and molded me to become the medium that I am today.

The Emergence of Spiritualism

Spiritualism was founded in America in 1848. It began when the teenage Fox sisters, Margaretta and Kate, experienced strange happenings in their small cottage home in Hydesville, New York. Disturbing noises, movements of objects, and other supernatural phenomena were happening day after day. Loud bangs and raps came from the walls, but they didn't seem to emanate from any specific point.

The girls decided to come up with their own form of communication to see if the noises would respond back to them. When the sisters began to clap their hands, the raps mimicked the same number of claps. They were highly perplexed, wondering if the noises and raps had some kind of intelligence. At one point, the sisters yelled out, "Knock twice for *yes* and once for *no!*" To their absolute amazement, they discovered the raps were answering them!

In earnest, they decided to devise another code, so they could communicate further. They came up with the idea of using raps to spell out the letters in the alphabet: one rap for *A*, two raps for *B*, three raps for *C*, and so on. The Fox sisters were very excited to come up with a way to have a conversation with whatever or whoever was rapping on the wall.

Through their new language, they discovered the noises were coming from the spirit of Charles B. Rosna. He said he was a traveling salesman who'd lived in their house a few years before, with a family named the Bells. Through a series of raps, Charles recounted how he'd been murdered and buried in the basement, and all his valuables had been stolen. He also told the sisters about a tin box that had been buried with him.

Eventually, the sisters' mom became aware of what they were doing. She wondered if this spirit could only hear her family, or whether he could see them as well. So, Mrs. Fox tried a little experiment. She clapped her hands *silently*, then asked the spirit to bang out how many times she'd clapped. To their amazement, the number of raps came back exactly the same.

The news of the sisters spread like wildfire, and people came from all over to experience the phenomena for themselves. One thing that people were amazed by was how *normal* the Fox sisters seemed to be. They were just simple folk with a basic education who were not particularly religious. From what everyone could see and experience, these girls were in fact communicating with the spirit of a man who had tragically died in that very house.

Of course, the story doesn't end there. The basement floor was eventually excavated. To no great surprise, the remains of Mr.

Charles B. Rosna, the traveling salesman, were found. Moreover, just as he'd told the sisters, there was the tin box lying right beside him. However, to this day, no one knows what was in the box!

The psychic happenings at the Fox home encouraged other people to try communicating with the Spirit World for themselves. Many homes across the country formed groups to attempt to communicate with loved ones who had passed. It was quickly discovered that some people were able to communicate with spirits far more easily than others, and soon mediumship was on the rise and Spiritualism was born. Many of its followers were women; it was the only religion where women could speak out and be heard.

Over the years, the Fox sisters went on to demonstrate their mediumship, talk about their experiences, and inspire others to believe. They helped others by using their unique form of mediumship in further attempts to communicate with other spirits.

While Spiritualism was founded in America, it really flourished in England. There are still Spiritualist churches in the U.S., but not nearly as many as there are "across the pond" as they say. Mediumship caught the attention of the British people, including royalty and even wise scholars and authors, such as Arthur Conan Doyle.

To this day, many continue their quest to learn as much as they can about this fascinating subject. I find it comforting that Spiritualism teaches us that God can be found in all things and that we're all connected. Since the spiritual force is in fact in all things, there can never be any discrimination. Spirit welcomes all. If we could all live with that belief, we'd all be better off for it.

DIFFERENT FACETS OF MEDIUMSHIP

Every one of us in this world is born with our own unique talents and abilities that we hope to use to influence and help others within our lifetime. Whatever our gifts — be it art, music, organizational skills, public speaking, writing, etc. — we all have something we do best, yet we're all uniquely different.

Just as each profession may have different specializations, the same goes for those who have a special gift when it comes to mediumship. We all vary in our ability, style, and skill. What one person may resonate with might not work for another.

Whether you're just starting to develop your own spiritual abilities or you're interested in going to see a medium, I want to make you aware of the different facets of mediumship. If you feel drawn to one of the following types of mediumship, I suggest you do your research. Get personal references through word of mouth, or try to see a medium who specializes in one of these types of mediumship in a public forum. No matter what you're searching for, the Spirit World knows how to reach out to you in any number of different ways.

Mental Mediumship

Mental mediumship is how I work. It is probably the most common form, the one you're most likely to have experienced in a private reading or seen onstage or on television. It's a mind-to-mind communication, also known as thought transference. In other words, it's mental telepathy, mind to mind between a spirit and a medium. Mental mediumship takes place via the consciousness of the medium, without using any physical senses; both the spirit and the medium blend their energy at the same frequency. Once the connection is made, the medium will verbally express or relay what they're receiving through their psychic senses. A medium who works this way will often receive factual information about who has passed, such as names, dates, how the person passed, places they lived . . . all without having any prior knowledge.

I discovered over the years that the best messages are given when I trust in Spirit and express *exactly* what I'm receiving. I've learned to not overanalyze the information, censor it, or put my own interpretation on it. I can't make the message about what I think *sounds* right; I just deliver it. Otherwise, I could possibly misinterpret what the spirit is trying to convey. I was taught some basic ground rules, which I now try to pass on to my students.

I learned wise words to live by during my training, namely: "Less of me — more of Spirit." There is no limit to what a medium can receive, but it depends on the quality and the receptivity of the medium and, of course, the Spirit Person who's sending the information.

Inspirational Mediumship

It's rare that a day goes by without some sort of random thought, idea, notion, or even a hunch that suddenly pops into your head. There's no rhyme or reason. You might be sitting in a coffee shop, or at the hair salon, or just having a soak in the bath. It doesn't matter where you are or what you're doing. Often, they come when you're not thinking or focusing about anything in particular.

Some believe that these inspired thoughts and ideas come from the Universe, God, a guide, or just from your own soul. They can equally be explained as part of a highly tuned intuition. For those who wish to play devil's advocate, it could be said that they're simply conjured up from your own mind or imagination. Some people spend a lifetime studying the wonders and miracles of the mind, asking themselves, "Where does it come from?" It's my belief that our spirit helpers often inspire us.

This is a type of mediumship that I experienced while studying in England. Then, I was part of an inspirational development circle where we sat in silent meditation to allow a spirit to draw close and blend with our own minds to impart inspired words. The circle leader who led the development group believed that, while it's helpful and healing to hear from your loved ones on the Other-Side with specific messages of hope, it's just as beneficial to hear inspirational wisdom from your guides who are much wiser and experienced. She said that it's often from such wisdom that true inspiration is born.

Inspirational mediumship is also known as *inspired speaking*. During an inspirational practice session while studying at the Arthur Findlay College in England, we were all told to reach into a box and randomly pick out a card. Each card was different, with just a single word written on it. We were already in a meditative state as, one by one, we each drew a card. We were told that as soon as we saw the word, we had to immediately begin speaking and allow ourselves to be inspired by the word.

When it came to my turn, I was amazed as the words just flowed. I knew the words were not coming from me, but it was as though they were coming *through* me. How do I know? Because the poetic words I was using and the grammar was not how I usually spoke, nor did I have the college or university training that would have enabled me to speak so eloquently. It was a great exercise to let go and trust in Spirit.

When you hear an inspirational medium or inspired speaker, it's almost as if the medium or speaker is talking directly to you. It's as if they know what you need and what's in your heart.

Healing Mediumship

Healing is the highest form of mediumship. As a medium, I've been blessed to witness healings at both a physical and spiritual level. During my years of intensive training, I studied various forms of healing, one of which was a form of spiritual healing. In many of the Spiritualist churches in the U.K., there are accredited healers who devote time to help people during the church service. I noticed that there were some common qualities that each healer possessed, such as generosity, compassion, and, most of all, love.

Love is one of the most important factors for the power to heal. In fact, love is the most significant and powerful force in our lives, whether it's loving ourselves or loving others. It comes from the deepest part of us and is part of our true essence.

During those healing sessions, which I was blessed to observe, people would arrange their chairs in a neat circle, the healer often standing silently behind them. The atmosphere was calm and serene; you could feel the energy of love flowing throughout the building. I sat and observed in silence, even though there was many a time I had to muffle a gasp or two. I witnessed images and lights that seemed to appear around the healers, and my heart was full because I was so grateful for the guidance and education I was gaining by simply being there and watching them.

"Can I place my hand on your shoulders and send you healing?" asked a healer. You could see the crippling pain etched all over the face of the man he spoke to. I sat there mesmerized as they both closed their eyes. It was an extraordinary sight, and I feel it doesn't do it justice to put it down in such simple words. The man's face relaxed as his excruciating back pain drained from his body. Although it lasted only a few minutes, I could almost see the healing power of Spirit flowing through the medium into this man. Tears ran down the man's face as his pain eased, and he left the service walking considerably straighter.

There's another form of healing that some mediums practice called *absent healing*. Spiritual energy combined with healing thoughts from the healer can be sent to a patient many miles away. There are no boundaries when it comes to sending healing energies of love and compassion.

I have seen many healers practicing different forms of spiritual healing, including Reiki, pranic healing, hands-on healing, Qi Gong, therapeutic touch, and even tai chi. One thing must be made perfectly clear here: energy does not come *from* the healer but *through* them. The role of a healer is to help their patients attune themselves to their *own* natural healing capacity. As Edgar Cayce said, "Spirit is seen as the God Force abundantly manifesting in the human body" and "true healing can be accomplished only when the spiritual nature of the human being is recognized as divine."

No healer should ever guarantee a cure. If you come across such claims, then I urge some caution. For a successful healing to take place, there's a set of conditions that any reputable healer would abide by. For example, they must be in good health themselves, both in body and mind. Equally, there could be a karmic condition, which could affect the outcome of the healing for the recipient. Healings don't always have an immediate impact and the full benefits are often felt over time. Remember that we're powerful beings and capable of miracles.

Psychic Art

Imagine going to a medium who is sketching away while they're talking to you, giving evidence that your mom is coming through. Then, when the session is over, the medium turns over their drawing pad and there's a perfect image of your mom! You not only walk away with the evidence but a special drawing that just further validates that your mom is still alive, happy, and healthy in the Spirit World.

Psychic artistry is one of my favorite forms of mediumship! There are many different ways that Spirit works through those who have this ability. Some psychic artists let Spirit control their hands as they draw. Others go into a deep trance and let Spirit completely take over, often with their eyes completely closed! Others see images in their mind's eye, and they simply draw what they're seeing without allowing their consciousness to attempt to influence or interpret what they think they should draw. Over the years, I've discovered that many psychic artists have little or no formal training; in some cases, they have no actual artistic ability at all. Yet, once the link is established, their artistic guide steps in to assist them in drawing works they'd never be able to do on their own.

I had the honor to have had a session with one of the most famous psychic artists in the world, the late Coral Polge, author of *Living Images*. (I wrote about her in my first book, *Born Knowing*.) To this day, I treasure the stunning pieces of artwork that she gave me at the end of my sitting. She must have drawn thousands of artworks in her lifetime. Her lovely colorful images of my Tibetan guide and family members have pride of place, adorning a wall in my private study.

Another psychic artist, friend, and colleague whom I've had the pleasure of knowing is Rita Berkowitz. I love watching her artistic magic come to life on the canvas. She's an amazing medium as well as a professional artist based out of New England. Watching her work and the way people's faces light up when she hands them their drawing is beautiful to witness.

I'm very drawn to this type of work, being quite artistic since my early childhood. Although I take the occasional drawing class in my spare time, I've never actually attempted to combine my artistic skills with being a medium.

Trance Mediumship

Trance mediumship is when a medium has the ability to enter an altered state of consciousness to allow a spirit communicator to use their body. It's almost as if the medium's own spirit steps back to allow a spirit to step forward to overshadow, influence, and control the medium. Since the spirit is speaking directly through them rather than the medium passing on information of what's coming to them, their voice and movements will be quite different from their own personality and character.

Most deep-trance mediums will not remember what transpired during a session and often have to be told when they come out of the trance. It's as though they have no conscious memory of what just transpired. There are various levels of trance control, from light to deep. A medium who works mentally (like myself) can be lightly entranced even though they're still present and remember everything. The blending may vary in both degree and level of intensity, but I think it's important to stress that a true trance medium will have studied and developed trance mediumship over a long period of time. They will also have worked very closely with their guides. There has to be complete trust to let a guide take control. It's essential for the medium to give their permission to the Spirit World as well as their guides to be used in this manner.

When I was developing my own mediumship, I studied the work of mediums from the past who were well known for their trance work, such as Emma Hardinge-Britten, Maurice Barbanell, Grace Cooke, Edgar Cayce, Eileen Garrett, Gladys Osborne Leonard, Leslie Flint, Ivy Northage, and many more. Many of these unique and special mediums subjected themselves to intense physiological and psychological experimentation in the hopes that it would shed some light upon the process of mediumship and psychic studies.

I believe that trance mediumship is making a comeback as I have witnessed some amazing mediums go into trance, where their voice, mannerisms, and language take on the characteristics of the spirit. Recently, I saw a medium work in trance, and it was so powerful that you could literally feel the energy shift in the room! When the medium stood up in trance, I could swear that, right in front of our eyes, he grew a few inches taller! It's hard to explain what we saw, but trust me I'm not one for making crazy statements or jumping to conclusions. I'm very supportive but equally careful when I see a medium work in any shape or form. The guide so entranced the medium's body that I believe we were witnessing his guide stepping forward.

I hope that you'll be able to see an authentic trance medium work for yourself. When you do, you'll feel it in your soul. It's such a powerful experience, it will touch your own spirit and heart. As always, trust your intuition and use your own discretion, while retaining your objectivity and discernment.

Physical Mediumship

The phenomena associated with physical mediumship are transfiguration, direct voice, levitation, apports (items that are brought through from the Spirit World), spirit lights, knocking and rappings, as well as materialization and dematerialization. However, this ability is rare to see these days. This unique type of mediumship had its heyday in the early 19th century, but too many people were taken advantage of because of rogues and charlatans who would falsify spiritual happenings under the cover of a darkened séance room. If you ever have a chance to see *real* physical mediumship, it's something you won't forget!

I was glad to hear that my alma mater, the Arthur Findlay College of Mediumship & Psychic Sciences, recently instilled a rule: If any trance medium is to demonstrate at the college, the medium has to allow night-vision glasses and infrared cameras to be used in the same room to uncover any trickery and ensure the integrity of the work. Darkened séance rooms are no longer allowed. In the past, many famous and reputable mediums allowed themselves to be tested within the scientific community such as Leslie Flint, Daniel Dunglas Home, Katie King, Mina "Margery" Crandon, Jack Webber, Leslie Flint, and Gordon Higginson.

Unlike mental mediumship, which can be developed and trained, physical mediumship requires certain elements that the medium must naturally possess within their body or vessel. One of these special elements is known as *ectoplasm*. The word comes from the Greek *ektos* and *plasma*, meaning "exteriorized substance." Ectoplasm has been described as the spiritual counterpart of protoplasm, which is the substance of a physical cell. Ectoplasm is a white substance that appears to stream out of the body of some mediums during a séance. It can come from any orifice, such as the ears, nose, eyes, mouth, or even the navel. It can form itself into a materialized spirit or part of a spirit, such as an arm, hand, or face in a materialization séance. It can also extrude from the medium's body and extend to support a trumpet or a levitating table. It is often accompanied by a slight smell of ozone.

———

The acceptance and belief that we do survive death is more prominent now than ever before. However, as with anything new, there are bound to be many questions: *Why am I here? Do I have a purpose? Can my spirit loved ones help me?* The answers to some of these questions can be found yourself when you connect with the Spirit World through meditation. A properly trained and experienced medium can receive answers because they're able to link to the spiritual realm effortlessly.

I hope you found this section interesting and that it provided you with some of the fundamentals and rudimentary knowledge of the different facets of mediumship. There is plenty of assistance out there, and who knows — maybe you have a specific interest in the abilities of mediums because you too have the same inclinations, even if you're not aware of them just yet.

Whether you're interested in exploring further, want to educate yourself of the subject of mediumship, or are searching for a medium because you feel ready to connect with a loved one, then I hope you go slow, do your homework, and find the right medium for you!

Chapter 6

CONSULTING A MEDIUM

Are you ready to see or consult a medium? Perhaps you're a little nervous, uncertain of the correct approach to finding and consulting one. This chapter is written from the perspective of helping those for whom it may be the first time they've considered seeing a medium.

There are many reasons people reach out to mediums, and these reasons are as different and varied as the people themselves. Perhaps you feel that those in Spirit World are trying to reach out to you. You might have already been the recipient of some after-death communications, or "calling cards" as I like to call them. Many people seek out mediums as a way to work through their bereavement due to the loss of a loved one. Some people are looking to resolve unfinished business, such as to give or receive forgiveness with someone who has passed on. Others visit a medium simply out of pure curiosity!

However, everyone has one thing in common . . . We're all seeking answers to something uniquely personal. The passing of a loved one or pet is one of the most painful and emotional experiences a person can go through in this life, and many of us have already experienced this. No matter your reason to seek out a medium, every session should be a healing experience and should always be treated as such.

WHEN SHOULD YOU CONSULT A MEDIUM?

The first thing you should decide is whether you need the assistance of a psychic or a medium. Many people who get the two confused will visit a medium in the hopes that their spirit loved ones can help them with their earthly concerns regarding their career, romance, or even finances. This is something that an authentic and trained psychic has the ability to assist you with. A medium, on the other hand, acts as the bridge between this realm and the next. (While I already wrote about the difference between mediums and psychics, I wanted to make sure this is explained again here because a reader might go right to this section before reading the book in its entirety.)

I always stress that you should only consult a medium after you had some time to grieve. I personally recommend a minimum of three months since a person's passing, as I believe this is a sensible period to wait; for some, however, it could take a little longer. Too many people want to run to a medium as soon as they lose someone, when in fact they're still in a state of shock filled with overwhelming sadness, which makes it hard for them to fully understand, appreciate, or even comprehend spirit contact.

This brings to mind a session that happened a few years ago, when two brothers came to see me with their mom. The men wanted to connect with their brother (the woman's son) who had passed away suddenly. As I sat down to begin the session, I could sense the person they desired stepping forward. However, when I looked up, I could see that the mom was so distraught. I could just tell from the look in her eyes that she was medicated. I knew that nothing I said or the messages that were starting to come through from her son on the Other-Side could have eased her pain at that moment.

All of a sudden, the woman began to wail uncontrollably that I had to end the session. To go on would have not served any purpose; in fact, it would have caused considerable pain all around, both to the immediate family and to her son in spirit. I didn't want to add to the mom's hysteria or depression, as she clearly was not taking in the information. As they were leaving, I pulled one of the men aside and asked him when they'd lost their brother. He told me that it had only been three weeks! Had I known, I would have never agreed to see them. Clearly, the event was far too raw for them.

Since then, I've learned how important it is to ask my private clients if they are seeking to reach out to someone who has *recently* passed and offer advice about the appropriate amount of time before seeing a medium. (When this particular session happened, my new assistant was just learning the ropes.) This waiting period is helpful not only for the sitter but also the person who has passed, because they need some time to reacquaint themselves in the Spirit World.

Some people feel that if they stop grieving, they are somehow letting go of their loved one. However, that's not the case; waiting and processing your grief doesn't mean you don't care or that you're letting go of your loved one. It's just that you're an intricate part of the mediumship session, and the medium and your loved one need you to try to be strong and present rather than still in that cloudy state of shock and bewilderment. It's important not to let the weight of the grief incapacitate you, as you play a key role in validating the information being relayed to you from your loved one or family on the Other-Side. Remember it's a three-way link — the medium, the spirit, and the recipient. When all three are in sync and in harmony, the magic of healing and the unbelievable feeling of pure love can be felt, and it can transform everyone involved!

FINDING A MEDIUM

There are so many mediums out there these days; the abundance of choices can be quite confusing. As always, I'm a big advocate of seeking a trained and experienced medium through word of mouth and personal recommendations. Most good mediums have a solid reputation, based on the strength of their evidence, their accuracy, and, of course, their compassion. I am *not* an advocate of just going to someone whom you've never heard of without a recommendation or at least the chance to watch them in person.

Every medium works in their own unique style. If you have a chance to see a medium of your choosing in person, onstage, or in a church, then I highly recommend doing so. You'll be able to see how they link with Spirit, the evidence and accuracy of what they're receiving, and the messages they receive from Spirit. But most important, you'll get to observe the process of healing that takes place. By going to see a medium work in a public setting, you'll have the chance to see whether you resonate with them, particularly if you're considering making a private appointment.

If you can't see a medium in your area, then you can see one of many mediums who offer private sessions over the phone or Skype — one of the great benefits of modern technology! It doesn't matter where a reading is done as, ultimately, it's just energy. It's a mental link, mind to mind. I don't need a person to be in front of me. Sometimes it's a benefit when I can't see someone, because then I'm not influenced by someone's body language or looks in response to anything I might say. I just focus on what I'm receiving from Spirit and the resonance of the voice at the other end of the phone.

Every time I demonstrate mediumship, whether it's onstage, at a smaller gallery session, or in a private reading, it's always unique and special to me. It can often be a life-changing experience for the person who's receiving a heartfelt message through a medium from their loved one. I so enjoy watching a mom smile or even laugh for the first time in months since she lost her child, or watching a husband shed a tear knowing his late wife wants him to be happy . . . For me, this is what mediumship is all about.

Another way to seek out a medium is to go to a Spiritualist Church, if there's one in your neighborhood. There's no reason to be nervous or worry that someone will try to convert you as soon as you walk in. At a Spiritualist Church, mediumship is demonstrated to confirm the continuity of life. You may enjoy a service, a lecture, a mediumship demonstration, and a healing portion that may follow the service. It's common to find a monthly "Medium's Day," where new and upcoming mediums will sit with you one-on-one. It gives mediums much needed practice in reading for individuals, and it's a good opportunity for you to slowly see how they work. These churches often bring in professional mediums from all over the world to demonstrate and teach. In the back of this book you'll find a resource list with a website that lists many of the Spiritualist Churches in the U.S. and other countries.

ADVICE FOR THE SEEKER

I've been on both sides — the medium as well as the sitter. I've come to realize that people have many varied expectations when visiting a medium, some of which have taken me by surprise and others which have touched my soul. I've had the honor of giving thousands of private sittings, so I would like to share practical advice to help you when you choose to sit with a medium. The information I'm providing here is the same I offer everyone who comes to see me for a session.

Whether you're having a one-on-one with a medium, participating in a group session, or seeing someone onstage with many other attendees, you'll quickly realize that every medium is different and has their own style of connecting with Spirit. The more you understand the delicate relationship between the medium, the Spirit World, and you, the better you'll appreciate the love and all that the Spirit World can provide when all three are in sync.

Those on the Other-Side want you to be happy! They want you to be successful and go on living, and they will do their best to show you how important this life is right now. What you do with the time you have here is very precious. I hope the following helps you to have an amazing session with a medium and, of course, your loved ones!

Research

Doing a little research on your friends and relatives who have passed makes it easier for you and the medium to understand who might be coming through so you can validate the evidence. Create a list of names, dates, geographical locations, circumstances of death, etc. You don't need to research your whole family and lineage, but those closest to your lifetime is good place to start.

Many people expect that a medium will bring through exactly whom they want, when in fact anyone can come through, even if you didn't know the person! For example, you might be visited by a grandparent who passed before you were born. Just because you didn't know them, it doesn't mean they don't know you. Our loved ones whom we know, as well as those we didn't know, are still our family and friends and connected to us. The person you hope will come through (at least when I'm working) usually does show up or make their presence known. Love is the bridge that allows your loved ones to draw close.

How the Medium Works

If this is the first time you're considering visiting a medium, it's wise to do your research so you approach the reading with a good understanding of what's likely to happen and the appropriate ways to respond. For example, if the person you are visiting has written a book, it's always worth reading that before your first session to get insight into how they work and their life as a medium.

If you have read this book in its entirety up to this point, then you understand that every medium has their own special ability in which they work mediumistically. This difference can affect how messages are received and understood — sometimes, with hilarious results!

I remember this time when I was sitting with a woman whose uncle was coming through. All he kept showing me was a child's toy rubber duck. It was quite bizarre, really, but I was not one to give up at the first hurdle. I asked her, "Why's your uncle showing me a rubber duck?"

The woman giggled and said, "My uncle's name is Doug. When I was a young child, I could never pronounce the name 'Douglas,' so I would say 'ducky.' For the rest of my life, he was always known as Uncle Ducky!"

I smiled back at her and let Uncle Ducky continue with his beautiful message. The Spirit World certainly does know how to get their evidence across.

People will often bring other people with them to their session, such as a best friend, a relative, or even a co-worker. But what people don't realize is that when you bring someone else to your session, you're opening the door for that person's friends or relatives to come through as well. Anyone who's present at the time could get a reading. I've had experiences with more than one sitter in which the friends' relatives dominate the entire session!

Another thing that can happen during a session is that you become the medium for someone else. What I mean is that your best friend's mother could come through to pass on a message to her daughter, even though you might not have known the mother. In that way, you end up being the conduit for that message. Why does this happen? In this case, the mom knows you're close to her daughter, so she's going to take any way she can to get her message through!

No medium can guarantee that they can bring a certain person through. Like I said, we don't have direct dialing to the Other-Side. If any medium says that they can, then I strongly recommend that you walk away. All we can do is our best — the rest is up to the Spirit World.

Have an Open Mind

Walking in with a healthy attitude and an open mind always helps the medium to ensure the session flows effortlessly. It really is all about energy. You must remember that mediums are psychically sensitive; the sitter's vibe and thoughts can affect a medium. There are times when people come to see me with a "prove it to me" attitude. This can create a wall that a medium has to break through before they even start.

I've come across sitters who feel they need to test the medium by thinking or asking specific questions, such as: "What's my mother's name?" "What did I bring of theirs that's in my pocket?" or "What's the code word my loved one and I had before they passed to prove they made it to the Other-Side?"

I always tell my sitters that if you have a specific question or a request from your loved one to prove themselves, then ask your loved one in your mind before you come to the session. When people ask me a question out loud, it can disrupt the link and cause me to slip back into my conscious mind. Of course, I'm not saying you *can't* ask a question during the session, but for me it can break the flow. If you don't understand a piece of information, the meaning could quite possibly be revealed or remembered at a later time.

I've received hundreds of letters and e-mails from people who've realized that the evidence given was correct, but they forgot at the time of the reading. On rare occasions, the medium may say something that doesn't immediately click or you don't know the answer. It's only when you go back and check the information as part of the validation process that you find out it was correct. I love when this happens, because some of the best mediumship evidence is something you didn't even know about. This just goes to dispel any myths that it's just about reading minds or pulling the information from you telepathically. I'd ask how can we pull out something that wasn't even in your mind? It's the wonders of how powerful the Spirit World can be!

Mediumship isn't a defined science because we're trying to link and blend with a spirit that no longer has a physical voice box to express themselves. They're sending their thoughts on a mental telepathic level, and it's up to us to interpret and decipher the meaning of what they're trying to convey.

On those rare occasions when I'm doing a reading, it does happen where no one will come through. Please know that it's not a sign that someone doesn't love you or that there's no one there. It could be any number of reasons, whether the medium is having an off day, the sitter may not be ready, or even that the spirit may not be ready to come through. Don't take it personally. Just know that it will happen when it is supposed to. If I realize after the first 10 or 20 minutes that I'm not linking with anyone, then I'll end the session at no charge and ask if they wish to try again with me in a couple of months. Usually when they come back, the link is created and they have a successful reading.

Don't Be Dependent on Mediums

When someone has a good session with a medium, they might then feel the need to go and see other mediums, one after the other. I have to say that this is really not a good idea on many levels. Hopefully, after a reading, you've heard what you needed to hear and felt there was some closure. It's important to then appreciate that your loved ones have their own lives now. Of course, they'll continue to be around when you need them and make their presence known when it's needed.

If you persist in visiting one medium after another, it's likely that your loved one will repeatedly come through with the same information. Why? Because it's like asking a relative to tell you about a trip they took. How many different ways can they tell you that story? When someone comes to see me for a private session,

I'll see them once, maybe twice at a push. After all, one of the recurring messages that spirits try to emphasize is that they want you to go on with your life until you see them again.

Furthermore, your loved ones are trying to send you signs themselves, but they're very subtle signs. So, if you're still feeling overly emotional or going through bereavement, it's possible to miss them. If your sense of loss is so great and you're missing them so much, then it's easy to miss feeling their presence. This is when a medium can be of great assistance and value to the people left behind.

The Medium's Responsibility

I believe that it's our responsibility as mediums to act as a bridge or conduit between the Spirit World and the living. It's our job to make you feel comfortable, especially if it's your first time. It's our job to explain how we work and, most important, what the sitter may expect. I strive to give the very best evidence possible that I'm receiving and bring through your loved ones in a way you can immediately recognize with whom I am linking.

As I said earlier, mediums should not be asking you for a lot of information. Usually, a simple "yes" or "no" or "I'm not sure" is all that's required to confirm or rebut the evidence. Also, do not feed the medium with information! Some sitters get so excited that they can't stop talking and end up giving away information about the person who passed. Remember, that's *our* job — not yours.

Mediums should be able to validate the spirit's presence with clear evidence. The basic foundation blocks of validation include: male or female, general age when they passed, what circumstances took them to the Spirit World, how they're connected or related to you, and so on. Once the identity is confirmed, the reading should get more detailed, and the medium might describe certain memories, places you visited together, birthdays, etc. There's no end to what type of information the medium might bring through. It can be a touching, loving memory or even an embarrassing moment to make you laugh and cry at the same time! After all, it's those special things that make them the person that they were — and still are.

————

There are many qualified and trained mediums that can be of service to the person that is bereaved and seeking answers. Take your time when looking for a medium. To recap: be open, try to understand the mechanics of how spirit contact works, and know that your loved ones never really leave you. They will do their best to reach out to show you that love goes on. They may contact you directly through signs and symbols, or through a medium. Over time, you'll know through your own inner knowing that the Spirit World is real, life goes on, and there is in fact an afterlife. Your grief and pain will lessen, knowing that there really is no death.

Part II

PSYCHIC AND MEDIUMSHIP UNFOLDMENT

Chapter 7

OPENING YOUR PSYCHIC AWARENESS

In today's society, most of mankind has forgotten what incredible, intuitive, sentient beings we are. Many of us have wandered too far into the realm of analytical thinking. We exist mainly in the physical world, which results in our focusing too much on everything that's outside ourselves. I think it's important, from time to time, to remember that there's a whole *inner world* ready and waiting for you that can be accessed whenever you want.

The entire second half of this book was written for people who want to understand and develop their psychic and mediumship potential. Whether you're just curious about what it takes or you have a desire to become a medium, I hope this section provides you with the guidance you've been seeking. Equally, if you're looking to understand the workings of your own spiritual abilities, then this part of the book will be of great benefit.

We all possess the spiritual ability to become more consciously aware of the inner workings of our soul, with all its capabilities and innate sensitivity. In other words, we have the natural capacity to utilize our intuitive psychic abilities in almost any area of our lives. One of my favorite statements to say during my presentations is: "We all came from God, and I don't think a Divine Intelligence would let us come here without a little help. The gift of intuition is our connection to the Divine." Although intuition is a gift that's given to each and every soul, it's important to remember that we're responsible for developing it ourselves.

When my students start exploring their psychic potential, they often ask me, "What's the difference between psychic ability and pure intuition?" There's a fine line between the words *psychic* and *intuition*, and the two are often used interchangeably. The use of one can often lead to the other, as a natural progression. Psychic ability is simply the *natural extension* of our intuition.

Most of us know what *intuition* means. How many times have you heard someone say, "I've got a hunch that . . ." or, "My instincts are telling me this . . ." or, "I have a strong gut feeling that . . ."? These are all forms of intuition. It's that hunch or that gentle nudge that so often comes out of the blue.

When we learn to *recognize, notice,* and *act* upon these feelings, we can establish a strong foundation for the development of our psychic abilities. Psychic ability is being able to take control of your intuition and make these special senses work *for* you. In fact, the word *psychic* is from the Greek *psychikos,* meaning "of the soul." This signifies that as spiritual beings, we're able to access, receive, and transmit information that reaches way beyond our physical body and our innate five senses.

Becoming aware of your psychic abilities is useful for more than becoming a medium or connecting to your loved ones. These abilities can greatly assist you in your personal and professional lives, as well as your relationships with family, friends, and colleagues. Opening the door to your natural psychic abilities is an exciting, enlightening, and life-changing experience. I've received thousands of letters and e-mails from past students who've told me that since they started working on their all-too-often-dormant abilities, they feel as if their soul or spirit is more consciously *alive* and *awake.* They say they're no longer sleepwalking through life.

I always enjoy teaching my psychic-development class (which is one of my signature workshops) because many who attend feel like they have little or no psychic ability when they arrive. But, once they go through the training and start to receive information via their psychic senses, the transformation is obvious. You can see it written all over their faces. It's almost as if they discovered something new, even though the ability has always been there, waiting to be accessed. Using your spiritual psychic abilities is quite natural. You can learn to recognize, practice, and trust those intuitive nudges more and more. By doing so, it becomes a wonderful resource for guidance, transformation, and self-empowerment that you can call upon for the rest of your life.

To live an intuitive or psychic life, you must first *believe* and *know* that you're already equipped with all the tools you need. As a spiritual being, you possess unlimited abilities, so it would be wise to acknowledge the potential that's waiting to be awakened, hence, my use of the term *dormant abilities*. The tools that help direct you to your inner guidance are your psychic senses — or, as I also refer to them, your "psychic strengths." To summarize, I'm talking about your inner feelings: *inner knowing* (clairsentience); *inner vision* (clairvoyance); and last, *inner hearing* (clairaudience).

As you sharpen and hone these senses, you'll learn how to work with the subtle energetic field (the aura), which surrounds everything and everyone. As you become more aware, you'll learn how to use the energy centers (chakras) of the body. (We'll discuss chakras in detail in Chapter 10.) This is all part of the necessary foundation for your mediumship unfoldment because it's through the psychic senses that you can pick up emanations that are given off or sent from the Spirit World.

BORN KNOWING

At one time or another, we've probably all had a psychic experience in our lives. Remember that we're all *born* psychic. It's as much your birthright as anybody else's. I believe that as children, we're all naturally intuitive. Have you ever watched a young child play, draw, or dance? It seems like they have one foot in this world as well as one in the next. They talk about things that we, as adults, don't readily see. They draw people in different shades of blazing color; I believe they are depicting the aura of the person without knowing it. So-called imaginary friends are often talked about, and many mothers mention having to set an extra place at the dinner table for their child's special invisible friend.

Children often talk about angels and how they see and experience themselves flying in their dreams. Some even have their own inner world that feels quite real and alive to them. They may also tell their parents for no reason if they like someone they just met, or if they don't have a good feeling about them. To them, it's quite natural to have such clear feelings, as nothing is clouding them, influencing them, or shaping them at such an early age. Children see the world as it really is and are very psychic because no one has had a chance to tell them they're not. But alas, as children enter their first years of school, the left side of the brain is awakened as they commence their education. They naturally pull away from the creative and intuitive right side of their brain as they start using the analytical left side of the brain for learning. It's all part of the educational phase of their young lives as they learn to spell, understand mathematics, history, and much more.

The result is that we pay less and less attention to our intuition to help guide us, and rely more and more on our physical senses to make decisions as we learn to rationalize and use logic. I find it fascinating that children who are raised in the Tibetan Buddhist tradition are educated from an early age about the spiritual energy systems of the human body and its chakra centers. How wonderful it would be if we did the same with our young in the West! The world could be a very different place, one of tolerance, shared values, patience, forgiveness, etc. Maybe in time, it'll be natural for children as well as adults to tap into this wonderful resource that's readily there for them — one that will help them navigate while they're on their path through life and always be a constant companion for their soul's journey.

RECOGNIZING YOUR PSYCHIC ABILITIES

To be intuitive or psychic is not just something we possess — it's more a way of being. This natural soul ability is not purely limited to transcended masters or to people who have devoted a lifetime of studying and practicing meditation. It's not about fortune-telling, crystal balls, or predicting the future. We're all using these special abilities most of the time, even though many of us don't realize it.

Put this book down for a few minutes and ask yourself:

- Have you ever just thought of someone and then run into them later that day?

- Can you sense the mood of someone even before you meet them?

- Have you ever had a hunch that you didn't follow through, only to later regret it because it was correct?

- Was there a time when you were talking to someone on the phone, and even though they sounded fine, you just knew that something was wrong?

- Have you ever known the outcome of a situation or an event before it happened?

- Can you walk into a room and tell what the atmosphere is like instantly?

- Do so-called coincidences and synchronicities keep happening in your life?

How many questions did you answer *yes* to? These are just a few examples of what being intuitive or psychic is all about. It's a sense of an inner awareness that can be quite subtle. (Once again, it's not overly dramatic like you see in the movies!)

I remember a time last summer when my intuition gave me a strong nudge that I couldn't ignore about my dog Koda. He can have issues with his teeth, and as a result, I've been diligent about his oral hygiene. During a routine check-up, when the vet looked at his teeth, she said we could wait until the fall to clean them. However, one evening soon after that visit, Koda was in his favorite spot on the couch and out of nowhere, I heard in my mind: *He has a bad tooth.* So I decided to take Koda back in for a dental cleaning as soon as possible instead of waiting until the fall.

After the visit, the vet called and said that the X-rays revealed an abscessed back tooth. It was infected and needed to be pulled immediately! By just looking at Koda's teeth, however, you wouldn't know anything was wrong; it took an X-ray to show what was happening inside. After discussing all the options with my vet, we agreed that the tooth had to come out to stop any pain Koda might be experiencing. He had the procedure and healed really well. The vet made sure she told me she was glad that I followed my instincts.

I may be a psychic medium, but even I don't always follow my intuition because, like I said, it can be so subtle that sometimes I think it's just a thought, or my imagination, or wishful thinking, rather than an intuitive nudge. But this time was different. Sometimes you have to trust what you're feeling, even when logic is pointing you in a different direction. By following your intuition, you'll be guided to make better choices.

Intuitive messages or nudges can happen anytime and anywhere. I recommend that you keep a small journal nearby to write down whenever you feel you are having an intuitive moment. Note any thoughts, visions, or feelings that you're having in that moment. I also try to notice when I receive a thought that has nothing to do with what's going on in my life at any one time. When that happens, I pause and ask myself whether it's an intuitive thought that I need to act upon.

So, the next time you think you're getting an intuitive thought or feeling, even if you're still not sure whether it's your imagination making it up, just pause for a moment and ask yourself: "Is this coming *to* me — or *from* me?" When you do this, you'll feel a strong sense of what to do next or which way to turn, and hopefully your intuition will add clarity for you. Remember that your imagination has a tendency to enter into your thoughts and leave, whereas a psychic hit or an intuitive nudge is more likely to keep coming back.

Here's a quick example: One day, all of a sudden, you have the thought to call your sister or another family member. You think, *I just talked to her last week, I'll call her later.* Several days go by and you get the thought again: *Call your sister!* Once again you tell yourself that you'll call later. The next day the thought comes back again, so you finally pick up the phone to call your sister, only to find out that in fact there was something wrong and your sister was so glad you called.

See, imagination will come and go, but a psychic impression or intuitive nudge will keep coming back. If you don't pay attention, it will get stronger or louder until you finally act on it. Trust your intuition, and it won't let you down.

THE BODY AS THE CONDUIT

Did you know that you're already equipped with a fundamental piece of equipment that will provide you with an endless supply of psychic information and guidance? You need look no further than your *own physical body* for answers. It really is this simple!

We're all constantly receiving information constantly via our psychic senses, but most people don't realize their body acts as a conduit in this process. Your body acts like one huge psychic antenna, operating at its own level of receptivity. Before you can use your abilities, you have to dedicate some time to becoming familiar and learning how to use the equipment — because you *are* the equipment.

Much research has been carried out as part of in-depth investigations into how our organs and glands play such a vital role in accessing psychic information. These organs and glands don't just work on a physiological level, they also act as receptors for information outside our physical world and help us access and receive psychic information. Some of these include the pituitary and pineal glands, heart, nerve endings, brain, and stomach. Basically, the *whole* body is being used in the process. Everything is made up of energy, including us, and it's important to value this precious commodity and to appreciate its effect on our total physical well-being.

Ancient Eastern and Western spiritual philosophies teach us about the universal life force that runs through everything, including *ourselves*. This spiritual energy breathes life into our bodies and keeps us connected to the Universal Force, which surrounds us all. Ancient Chinese medicine has its own unique name for this universal energy that flows through us, *chi*, or what the Hindus call *prana*. It surges through our vital organs and permeates our bones, our bloodstream, and other parts of the body along a network of internal systems called *meridians*.

This *spiritual energy* is what healers and other natural health practitioners, such as acupuncturists and massage therapists, work with. Often, they work to remove blockages in our energy system to enable the energy to flow freely. When blockages in our energy system are ignored, they can manifest as ailments such as aches and pains, or they can create imbalances in our mental and emotional states. Keeping the energy flowing smoothly throughout our system promotes a healthier mind and body.

THE IMPORTANCE OF LEARNING THE EQUIPMENT

Your body has a way of sending you signals through its own psychic language. Whether it's a gut response, a physical sensation, an emotion, or even a dream, your body is talking to you!

I got my first real lesson in listening to my body when I was involved in a near-fatal automobile accident, which I wrote about in my first book, *Born Knowing*. The shock to my system from the accident resulted in my energy centers (better known as chakras) being forced open. Up to this point, I had so often pushed my abilities away, but now they were back with a strength and intensity I'd never experienced before. Still, I didn't want to just casually accept this ability without some clear framework of understanding and appreciation. I had to know how and why this was happening, but more important, I needed to know whether or not I could control it. After the accident, I poured myself into studying everything I could read about the vital energies in and around the body. (But you don't have to look outside yourself for the answers or get into an accident to be psychic!)

We generally don't pay enough attention to our bodies or heed their signals until something goes wrong. That's why it's so important not to push your physical sensations or feelings away during the process of your psychic development. Embrace them and listen to them. When you use meditation, you'll be able to find the answer to what your body is trying to say — so just ask. You may not get anything at first, but it's worth persevering, as it really does get easier with practice.

To ignore your body or your feelings is to ignore your intuition. For example, I know from my own experience that when I dream of being immersed in water up to my chest, it's often symptomatic of the onset of bronchitis, so I take greater care and ensure I dose up with vitamin C as a precaution. In other words, I *acknowledge* and *act* on the warning signs.

Taking care of your body and your health should be a top priority, especially when you're developing your psychic and mediumistic abilities. Ultimately, *you're* responsible for your physical health. I believe it's essential to follow a sensible regime of balance and moderation. Eat a sensible diet, drink plenty of water, and take a good daily vitamin, rest (as well as sleep), and exercise. If you have a clean and healthy body, you stand a better chance of reducing those "blocks." This will greatly help you in becoming more receptive.

THE PRICE OF SENSITIVITY

I always tell my students to ingrain the following words into their minds: The price of sensitivity . . . is sensitivity.

Remember that doing psychic work can make you *extra* sensitive, so you may occasionally feel tired or drained. Being sensitive comes with this work, and one of the most common sayings I hear from my colleagues is: "It's part of the job." If you weren't highly sensitive, you wouldn't be able to reach or be aware of the Other-Side too easily.

It's not uncommon for many sensitive people to also have anxiety, and anyone who knows me well knows it goes without saying that it can affect me from time to time. Growing up in an alcoholic home, I've come to understand that "worry" as a child turns into *anxiety* as an adult.

For me, it's been a lifelong balancing act between taking care of myself and being a professional medium. There's a lot of energy running through my body at any given time; when I'm ramping up for a demonstration, it can be extreme. I have to manage this delicate balance for myself, so that my health and overall well-being are not compromised. Now I'm not saying that everyone who suffers from anxiety is necessarily a psychic or medium, and I always recommend that anyone who's constantly anxious contact a doctor or therapist for help.

It's important to relieve yourself of tension and stress, whether through massage therapy, yoga, meditation, or physical exercise. Find out what works best for *you* and try to add it to your daily routine. Get out in nature and go for long walks in the woods or at the beach. Breathe! Mother Nature is a wonderful healer. Most important, remember to close down your chakras. (I'll show you how to do so in Chapter 10.)

When working with your intuitive abilities, it's perfectly okay if it gets to be too much, so just take a break from your training for a few days or however long you need. You're here in the physical world, and you have to stay balanced and grounded with your physical life as well as your spiritual life. Honor your equipment. The physical body is *not* just a vehicle to get you around while you're here on earth; it's meant to assist you while your spirit is living in it. Hopefully, you'll never look at your body in the same way again. Know how special *you* and *your body* are — get to know each other.

WE ARE ENERGY

Receiving psychic information is all about *energy*. Everything is made up of energy. People, spirit beings, places, and even objects store energy. Since you too are energy, you can receive and read information via your psychic senses. Being psychic is like a television. We all know that you cannot see TV signals through the airways (as they're vibrating at such a high frequency), yet we know they're being transmitted. Our television sets receive these signals, and in a way, they're descrambled to form a picture on our screens. So, it's the same logic when it comes to psychic energy. We receive information constantly through our psychic senses and the result is an impression or feeling that we didn't receive via our physical senses. As we develop our psychic strengths, we get better at descrambling and making sense of the signs and symbols.

When training to use your psychic ability or mediumship, you must realize you're also training your conscious mind to receive thoughts and information in a way that it's not accustomed to, so it's good to give it some guidance by affirming: "I am psychic, and it's natural for me to receive words, images, and feelings beyond my normal ability."

I've always gone to great lengths to explain the mechanics of how psychic ability works and the varying levels of its receptivity. It's important to me that others are reassured of the authenticity and legitimacy of this work. I learned much of this while training in the U.K. and educating myself with the work of the late Ivy Northage, a famous medium whose work always resonated with me. I so wish I'd had the opportunity to meet her while she was alive. I heard from some of my colleagues who were fortunate to have studied with her that she was quite a force and an unbelievably tough teacher. One of Ivy's great sayings was: "When you accept and believe in your psychic abilities and yourself, your mind will be open to receive the mental training that your development will provide."

Over the years, I've learned and now believe that there are three types of psychics: those with an uncontrolled ability, those who are partially developed, and those who have recognized their potential and are in control of their abilities. To provide a little more of an explanation, here's a longer description of each level.

- **Uncontrolled Ability:** These are people who are psychically sensitive and don't even know it. They respond on an emotional level and are an open beacon to the Spirit World, to other people, and to the stimulation of the outside environment. They may not feel comfortable in large crowds. They are empathic, picking up on the emotions of others, and they can sometimes feel emanations from the Spirit World.

- **Partially Developed:** People at this level usually have little or no knowledge of the mechanics of their ability or how it works. They have difficulty discerning genuine psychic ability from their own thoughts. They might have read or studied a little on the subject, but never continued their education or practiced using their abilities.

- **The Masters:** This is what I hope every student strives for. People who work at this level are those who appreciate the mechanics of their psychic faculties and understand how to work in partnership with Spirit. They're in control of their abilities at will, and are trained, qualified recipients of spirit communication. They are the masters of their abilities; their abilities are not the master of them.

When I hear stories from students saying that the Spirit World is always bothering them, it tells me that they have not yet learned how to close themselves down by using their chakras (which you'll learn in Chapter 10) or how to withdraw their aura (which you'll learn in Chapter 9). In other words, they still haven't mastered their abilities. As I've been doing this work for many years, I'm able to detach myself from being constantly linked with the Spirit World when I'm not working as a medium. It would take a very strong or persistent spirit to get my attention when I'm not working. When it does happen, it's usually because I have an event coming up, and it's quite natural for them to start blending with my energy. In that case, I just say to them using my thoughts: *See you at the event!* Of course, if there's an important message or a warning of some sort, I might not have a choice — some spirits can be quite determined!

For instance, as soon as this man walked into the room at a party I was invited to, I just knew that his brother (who had passed) was with him. I wasn't at a spiritual party or a group reading or anything like that. I'd attended this get-together for computer software technicians with a friend; otherwise, no one knew who I was.

So, there I was, not really knowing the right thing to do in this situation. I didn't want to walk up to the man and say, "Hi, have you lost a brother?" and launch into a full-blown reading. That would have probably freaked him out. Furthermore, I'm not an advocate of walking up to people and giving them messages, because I'm never sure of their faith or their personal beliefs, nor would I want to impose on their privacy or emotions suddenly. It's just not good ethics; I respect the Spirit World, but I also have to respect those here.

Instead, I sent out a thought: *If you want me to give your brother a message, then you figure out how that's going to happen.*

A message *wasn't* given that night! However, you can trust that when a spirit wants to give a message to someone, they'll figure out how best to do it and the appropriate time and place. I hope the man's brother in spirit was able to guide him to someone who could give him a message.

If you feel your calling is to become a psychic or a medium, then I encourage you to really study. It's essential that you learn how to use your psychic and mediumship abilities, as well as understand the mechanics of how it all works. Also, there are ethics (listed in Chapter 11) that any good medium will practice; doing so ultimately makes you a more confident and respected medium to those here as well as those on the Other-Side.

Talking about practice, I'd like to share with you the following exercise, which is great for beginners.

Beginners' Psychic Exercise

Using your psychic ability is just the same as using any muscle in your body: You have to use it to strengthen it. This exercise, which I often use in my workshops, can be very helpful and fun to do. I ask someone to pretend they're already psychically aware. They then choose someone else in the room that they feel naturally drawn to. They're instructed to give off any information they're receiving, even if they feel they're making it up.

When you're feeling free, there's no pressure to be right, and you have fun doing it! In this case, your imagination and psychic ability work hand in hand to create a natural flow of information. It's not uncommon for the spirit of a loved one to slip into your mind when you're not pressured to perform or to be accurate.

Of course, what often happens is that everyone thinks they're making it all up, only to learn later that they received some accurate information. While there might be as many misses as there are hits, the students and the rest of the class are pleasantly surprised by just how much accurate information is actually given. This is because they're having fun and letting themselves have free rein without expectations.

Here are some simple actions you can try as part of your own development:

- Before you sit down at your desk in the morning, ask yourself: "How many e-mails will I receive today?" or "What will my boss be wearing today?"

- When the phone rings, see if you can *sense* who's on the other end, before you look at the caller ID.

- When receiving utility bills, try to *guess* the amount before you open the envelope.

- If you're at a building that has multiple elevator doors, stand in front of the one you *feel* will open first.

- If you're feeling confident, see if you can *visualize* a word or two from tomorrow's newspaper headlines.

As you're practicing and developing, it's important not to get hung up on whether you were right or wrong. Making the effort is the important part; it will have great value as you discover how your intuition or psychic ability receives and interprets information. As I end this section, it's important to repeat that everyone works with their intuitive psychic abilities in their own way, so you should never try to emulate someone else.

RECORDING YOUR PROGRESS

Earlier, I talked about setting aside a special room for yourself — a room that will assist you in quieting your mind and, in turn, allow you to go into stillness. This special room or sanctuary can also be where you go to study your psychic work.

As well as creating this dedicated area for yourself, I highly recommend you keep a journal to record your psychic thoughts, your dreams, and your impressions. You may decide to have more than one journal in different locations so that no matter where you are, you'll have a place to record your progress, along with those intuitive flashes and impressions. (You can also use an app on your phone or other personal electronic device.)

Remember, psychic thoughts can happen anytime, anywhere! Your journal will become a valuable resource both now and in the future as you look back on your progress. It will offer great insights of when you were right or wrong, and who knows, it may even become a teaching manual in itself. I have journals that go back years in which I recorded hunches, impressions, exercises, and, of course, my dreams. When I look back through them today, I can see how my abilities have strengthened, how they have grown and become clearer and more integrated with the rest of my physical being. In fact, some of the teaching methods that I use today come right from those very journals!

Tips for Your Psychic Journal

If you're about to start your first journal, make sure that you record your entries with a time and date so that you can see your progress when you look back days, months, and years later.

Here are a few ideas that you may want to put in your psychic journal.

- Any unexpected thoughts or impressions that come to you that seem to be outside of your day-to-day routine, even if you feel that you're making them up

- Coincidences and synchronicities that seem to continually run through your life

- Identical numbers that keep showing up in your life, whether you see them on license plates, clocks, phones, etc.

- Dreams, images, and emotions that you're able to remember from your sleep

- Any pictures or symbols that come into your mind (try not to edit what you're receiving)

- Your personal goals and desires

- Affirmations that really inspire you (or make up your own)

Just the process of keeping a journal in itself will help your consciousness expand because you're starting to work with and getting to know your own inner guidance system. This will lead to a gradual awakening as you start to notice how your mind and spirit are working together to interpret the language of your soul.

Chapter 8

YOUR PSYCHIC STRENGTHS

Each and every one of us is born with our own unique set of individual gifts, talents, and abilities. Just as some of us have the ability to be artists, teachers, construction workers, personal trainers, or authors, the same can be said for one's ability to be psychic.

After studying psychic awareness and mediumship for more than two decades, if there's one thing I've learned it's that we all possess some psychic ability, and each of us works in our own special way depending on that psychic ability. I like to teach my students to have a solid foundation and understanding when it comes to the mechanics and inner workings to strengthen their core psychic abilities. I teach people how to use them in their everyday life, including their home life, work life, social life, and their personal relationships. Once you start using your unique psychic ability, it will help you to practice when it comes time to explore your mediumship potential. I encourage my students to become completely educated and comfortable in the way they use their psychic abilities before we move on to the teachings of mediumship, because it's through their psychic senses that mediumship will be accessed and used.

Although there are a wide variety of psychic abilities, for the purpose of this book, I want to focus on the three most popular, which you'll be able to access once you've identified your individual psychic strength. These abilities are known as clairsentience, clairvoyance, and clairaudience. When I'm working as a medium, Spirit People will use me as their instrument to communicate in any number of ways, but usually it's the strength of my clairsentience and clairvoyance that provides the best outcomes and the clearest messages.

UNDERSTANDING YOUR OWN STRENGTHS

When you watch a psychic or medium work, you can get a good indicator of their psychic or mediumistic strength just by listening to the words they use as they're working. You'll often hear them say, "I'm *feeling* or *sensing* . . ." (clairsentience); "I'm being *shown* . . ." (clairvoyance); or "I'm *hearing* or *being told* . . ." (clairaudience).

It's quite natural that some of you will already know where your core psychic strengths lie. For example, if you think your individual psychic aptitude is to become a *feeler*, then you should work to strengthen your clairsentience before you start developing your other psychic senses. I've noticed that many students who participate in my workshops start off with the belief that clairvoyance is the best way to receive psychic information. However, being a good clairsentient can also produce excellent results. With time and practice, as well as some patience, it will be possible to use all three of these primary psychic senses so they work in harmony and unison. By discovering which is your primary strength at first, you'll be able to begin building a solid foundation with your own individual psychic self and become highly tuned and more receptive, which is needed for mediumship.

If you choose to move on to developing your mediumship potential, then be open and flexible and see what strengths start to develop and grow stronger, that way the Spirit World will use you in *their* way. It's likely that your strengths will pass from one phase to another. All my "clairs" are used in my mediumship now, whereas before, clairsentience was my dominant strength. Spirit knows your strengths and weaknesses, and I think it's a good thing to send out this thought once in a while to Spirit: *Use me, but use me in* your *way, not mine.* If anything, it will keep you humble and open to the opportunity for your mediumship to continually grow and evolve.

It's also important to remember that you should never emulate the way another psychic or medium works. Why? If you think about it, doing so means that you'll only be coming in second best to the original. Some students may see a popular medium and try to mold their mediumship around the way the person they admire works. By doing so they're impeding their own mediumship unfoldment, the potential for growth, and the opportunity to enhance their own acute senses of awareness. Be yourself. Don't try to mold yourself or force your abilities; by doing so you're doing yourself a great disservice.

TRUST IN SPIRIT

As my own abilities have grown and changed over the years, sometimes all three of my psychic strengths are used at once, depending on the Spirit People's needs when I'm receiving and relaying a message from them. I just keep myself open and ask them to use me in their way as opposed to mine. I put my total trust in the Spirit World. They know what they're doing, and in my case, a large crowd never daunts them!

A few years ago, I was giving a keynote lecture and demonstration for my publisher, and the audience was packed to capacity with more than 2,000 people. I didn't realize at the time that my lecture was going to be simultaneously broadcasted live online for the people who couldn't attend the event. As I heard my name, I stepped onstage into the spotlight and immediately noticed the lighting was dimmed over the audience to a point where I could hardly see them.

I whispered to the event organizer backstage, "Please turn up the lights, I like to see the audience." I waited, and still the audience was in semidarkness. I could feel the audience in front of me anxiously waiting for me to begin, so I asked again. "Please turn up the lights."

The producers whispered loudly through the backstage curtains: "We can't! It's a live broadcast, and we need the lighting this way so the people at home can see you with just the stage lighting."

I didn't panic or yell. I just put the thought out quickly to the Spirit People, *Well, what are we going to do?*

All of a sudden, I could sense that my clairaudience had been switched on, as though someone had turned up the volume to max! That day, I did the whole 90-minute lecture and mediumship demonstration using my clairaudient strength. Words came clear and fast from the Other-Side as they described themselves, how they'd passed, names, as well as geographical locations of where they'd lived. I got details about their hobbies and the relationship they'd had with the members of the audience. As each spirit was identified, verified, and accepted by an audience member, the information just flowed. What was doubly unusual and somewhat disconcerting with the dim lighting was that I couldn't see any of the audience members talking back to me. I just had to totally rely on my clairaudience, listening to the voices of the Spirit People as well as the responses from the audience. This was pure clairaudience at it's very best, and a day I won't forget for a long time! I can't take all the credit — I'm just the vessel, not the one working behind the scenes. Those on the Other-Side also deserve the applause that day!

The Spirit People knew that day that I didn't have the opportunity to see the audience or work in my usual way, so they took over. I remained calm, as I just knew they wouldn't let me down or disappoint the couple thousand people hoping for a message from their loved ones. In this case, I just got out of my own way and put my trust in Spirit.

As I've said, it's good to know as you start your development where your psychic strengths may be strongest, but please try not to lock yourself into one. Give yourself the freedom to discover and understand the workings and mechanics of all of them. In the future, you too will learn and grow in ways you never thought possible.

Now let's explore and understand the workings of the three major abilities, and discover just how many you actually possess.

CLAIRSENTIENCE, OR "CLEAR FEELING"

Clairsentience is the inner sense of *knowing*. This is one of the more familiar intuitive senses, and it's probably the easiest one to develop and access. For example, have you ever walked into a room where an argument has recently taken place, and you could actually *feel* it? Do you know why?

When energy lingers, you end up sensing the emotions and conditions that led to that argument through your clairsentient ability. In other words, you're *feeling* the turbulent, negative energy of that recent argument.

Here's another example. Let's say you're introduced to someone for the first time at a social gathering, and you immediately get that feeling of discomfort or uneasiness. It's not so hard to grasp what you're sensing. You just *know* you're not really going to bond with that person. It's a gut reaction, but we tend to rationalize it by telling ourselves that we probably won't have anything in common with them. What's actually happening is that you're receiving thoughts and feelings from that person's aura, which are then transmitted through your solar-plexus chakra, which is in the abdomen area. (In Chapter 10, we'll be going into detail about the seven major chakras and their associations with your "clairs.") This results in what we so often call that "gut feeling," which in this case is a form of clairsentience.

Consider the following questions. Each *yes* is a strong indicator of clairsentience:

- Are your feelings easily hurt?

- When meeting someone, do you intuitively know when something's wrong, even though they appear to be happy?

- When you're driving, do you instinctively sense when you should take a particular route, only to find out later that there was a terrible traffic jam on your original route?

- Are you the person who everyone goes to when they're feeling down, or when they need to get something off their chest?

- When you walk into a room do you just *feel* whether the placement of the furniture is correct or not?

- Have you noticed people are simply drawn to you? Do people often come up to you and ask for directions? Also, when you're shopping in a store, do people think you're an employee and ask you questions?

These are just a few of the possible signs of a clairsentient's sensitivity.

People are naturally drawn to clairsentients. Many people who are *feelers* will also receive other people's stuff. By "stuff," I mean information that's not yours. If your natural psychic inclination is to *feel*, it's more than likely that you'll pick up vibrations from other people, which can affect your disposition.

There's a cautionary note that I need to make here. If you're clairsentient, it's likely that you'll pick up other people's emotions, whether happy or sad. If your temperament is usually one of an upbeat personality, and for some inexplicable reason you start feeling down (even though there's nothing happening around you to cause this), try approaching it from a different angle. Instead of wondering, "What is wrong with me?" ask yourself, "*Who* is wrong with me?" You're probably tuning into feelings or vibrations from someone else, without even knowing it. Your psychic ability can and wants to help.

Next time this happens, stop for a few minutes and focus on your solar-plexus chakra and ask yourself, "Whose feelings are these?" As you do this, see if an image of someone comes to mind. It could be anyone, from a member of your family to a best friend, neighbor, or even a co-worker. Try calling them and casually ask how they are. You may be surprised to find out that they're the one who's feeling down.

We live in a society that's less prone to hugging, touching, or embracing each other. A clairsentient *needs* to touch and feel things physically. This benefits your intuitive psychic ability and helps you understand someone on a much deeper soul level. In other words, you'll be making a *soul-to-soul* connection.

The hands are wonderful receptors of energy. The next time you meet someone new, look into their eyes, reach out, shake (and hold) their hand, and make a *real* connection. Equally, when you meet a friend, give them a big hug. Just being aware of your clairsentience and the subtle ways you receive information will help you in so many ways and provide a wonderful tool to help find the answers to those unanswered questions.

Clairsentience on a Mediumship Level

When a medium is working using their ability of clairsentience, they'll be able to *feel* or *sense* the spirit's energy, whether it's male, female, young, or old, and where their illness was in the body that might have taken them to the Other-Side. The medium will describe the spirit's personality, get a sense of their mannerisms, and, in some cases, take on the characteristics of the spirit. This is the most common way most mediums work, and there are no limits to what the spirit can make the medium sense.

When a spirit draws close to me and blends with my aura, I might start talking and walking like them, maybe even taking on some of their characteristics, such as a nervous twitch or a facial expression that they were known for while here in their physical body. It's always a joy to see the look on the recipient's face as they begin to witness their loved one's true personality and character communicate by using me as their vessel. It's almost as if their loved one is right there in front of them. In reality, on a spiritual level, they are!

I was also taught that as a medium, I can enhance my blending with a spirit even more by asking them to come close and merge with my aura, almost as if they're stepping into my shoes. It's like I'm looking through their eyes and becoming them. When I'm working clairsentiently with someone who has passed, I now practice something I was taught very early on, namely: less of me — and more of the spirit.

Exercise: Opening Your
Psychic Sense of Clairsentience

You can use your psychic strengths for a whole host of reasons. If you're preparing to make an important decision, whether it's about a new relationship or business, buying a new car or home, or changing jobs, focus on your clairsentient conduit — your solar-plexus chakra — and try the following exercise.

Start by settling yourself in your personal space. Close your eyes and hold your hands gently over your solar plexus area. Imagine this area of your body is slowly filling up with beautiful yellow light.

When you feel settled and comfortable, ask yourself: "How do I feel about this decision?" or "How do I feel about this person?"

See if a feeling or an image comes to mind. Ask yourself: "Does it feel positive or negative?" If you feel uneasy about what you're feeling, then ask again: "Why am I uneasy?" The more specific the question, the more specific the answer is likely to be. This exercise only takes a few minutes and can provide some really helpful insights!

Additional Clairsentience Exercise

Here's another great exercise that has saved me a lot of time from unnecessarily blaming myself for other people's actions. When you sense or feel a negative mood emanating from someone, you can use this technique to understand what's going on with them — before you blame yourself.

The first thing you need to do is get *yourself* out of your own way. Discard the thoughts relating to what you're perceiving or feeling. Relax, close your eyes, and breathe.

Try to imagine that you're literally stepping into the other person's shoes and becoming that person. Feel what they're feeling. See if you now have a better understanding of what's *really* happening and how you could possibly help.

———

Now that you have the rudimentary basics about clairsentience and know how to access this ability, use it to experiment in any area of your life you feel could benefit. This ability can become highly tuned; if necessary, you can turn it down to decrease your psychic sensitivity by focusing on your solar plexus and imagining the yellow light getting smaller. Once you've practiced working with your clairsentience, try going for walks in the country and opening yourself up to *feel* the outdoors in all its beauty. Since everything is made up of energy, you'll quickly learn to feel it all.

CLAIRVOYANCE, OR "CLEAR SEEING"

Clairvoyance is the inner sense of *seeing*. It's when you receive images, pictures, symbols, and colors. It's important to note that this is not about seeing in the physical sense with your eyes; it's about using your *inner eye*, better known as "the third eye." I believe that the soul never speaks without a picture.

Don't let any of the popular misconceptions of clairvoyants hinder your personal development. We all know that some people can find the unknown a little scary, and the power of the rational mind can be a strong deterrent at times. The word *clairvoyant* itself can even be off-putting. It's easy to be influenced by television shows, which stereotypically portray clairvoyants with those cliché-ridden images, such as smoke-filled rooms with hands clasped around a crystal ball. I think it's time to dispel those myths.

I once heard a wonderful story from a lovely couple that expresses how clairvoyance can be an everyday experience. While sitting in his living room, Jack looked up at a newly bought picture of an angel that his wife had proudly hung right over their fireplace. While staring at this new piece of art and trying to figure out whether he liked it, Jack noticed the face of the angel begin to blur and change. A new face was taking shape and transforming right in front of him. He blinked a few times to see if his vision would clear, but the image before him continued to change. The angel was starting to resemble his aunt Mary, whom he had not seen for some time. Of course, he told himself that he was seeing things and put the experience down to his imagination. He'd had a long day, so he just assumed he was tired. Well, that's what his rational mind told him. After all, he wasn't into all this "stuff," he jokingly explained to me while telling his story.

The next day, Jack was perplexed, as he couldn't get the image of his aunt's face out of his mind. He called up his cousin Carol, Mary's daughter, and warily told his story to her. He knew that Carol was more aware and open to metaphysical phenomena such as this. Now Carol knew for a fact that Jack was not into telling stories, so as soon as he'd hung up, she called her mother to see how she was doing. "Mom, it's Carol. I know this sounds weird, but I'm just calling to make sure you're feeling okay?" Her mom told her that she was fine but explained that she had been feeling a little dizzy lately. Carol decided to take her for a checkup the next day, just as a precaution.

Well, I think you know where this story is going. The doctor ran all the usual battery of tests and found that Jack's aunt Mary had abnormally high blood pressure and needed medication immediately. Due to Jack's clairvoyant image and the actions that followed, his aunt was able to get to the hospital before her health deteriorated.

Consider the following questions. Each *yes* is a strong indicator of clairvoyance:

- Do you often experience vivid, highly memorable dreams?

- Do you have a natural eye when it comes to placing furniture to enhance the energy flow or the aesthetics of a room?

- Have you ever looked at someone and known they were coming down with an illness, even though they appeared quite healthy?

- When talking to someone on the phone, are you able to envisage what they look like, even though you've never met?

- Have you ever looked at something, whether it's a painting, a piece of wood, or even a cloud, and ended up seeing other images within the object you're viewing?

Clairvoyance is just seeing through your mind's eye. To be a little more scientific, the reception area for this ability is situated in the third-eye chakra (between your brows), and its associated with the pituitary gland. People who display a strong tendency toward being clairvoyant often want to spend time in big, open, well-lit spaces. Equally, when they travel, they're the ones who have to see it all, as though they can't bear to miss anything! As with clairsentience, using your clairvoyant ability can benefit you and others, once you know how to access the specific reception area and interpret your own symbols and images.

In the early stages of development, many students tell me how images and symbols that they receive can be fleeting and quite subtle. If you're not a trained psychic or medium and you lack a heightened psychic awareness, it's quite possible that you wouldn't even notice such images or symbols, as they're easily missed. This is where the practice of mind focus will greatly help your clairvoyance. Another popular misconception I've heard is that some people think that a 3-D rift will open up right in front of them with a clairvoyant image. In reality, the truth is a lot less dramatic in that it's more about receiving symbols or images and sometimes words.

Each of us has our own unique interpretation of symbols, and what an image or symbol means to one person can have a totally different meaning to someone else. Over time and with practice, the same symbols will repeatedly come back to you clairvoyantly, and you'll learn how to interpret them by drawing your own analogies and personal reference points. It's important to make a note of these symbols in your journal so you understand their relevance and importance. Ask yourself: "What does this image mean to me?" Once you become proficient with your clairvoyance and you've built a good psychic database of images, then these familiar words will totally ring true: "One picture speaks a thousand words!"

A great way to train and sharpen your clairvoyant ability is to listen to meditation tapes that use visualization techniques that take you on a beautiful journey in your mind's eye. I also recommend that whenever you spend time outside, try to notice everything around you, whether it's the deep blueness of the sky or the calming greenness of the grass and trees. Try to notice all the diverse cultures of people you're exposed to every day. So many people, when they're developing this ability, want to see with their psychic eye immediately, whereas I believe it's important to start by looking and noticing the surroundings right here in the physical world. If you follow my advice, you'll be training your eyes and your mind to notice more. This will assist you in developing your clairvoyant strength.

Clairvoyance on a Mediumship Level

Many psychics and mediums see subjectively — in other words, in their own mind. Sometimes you may notice a psychic or medium looking away or just beyond the sitter when they're giving a psychic reading, which is quite natural. For example, when I create a link with the Spirit World, I'm well known to look and put my awareness to the left side of me, even though nobody is physically there. It's not like I don't want to make eye contact with the sitter; it's more that I'm reaching out and blending with the energy I am feeling or experiencing. I refer to it as my "psychic screen," and for me, it's almost as though a mini-movie is playing out, right in front of me. Over the years, I've honed this skill and developed the ability to see the images with greater clarity and definition.

On a mediumship level, when a medium is using their ability of clairvoyance to work with a spirit, the person who has passed will send visual images to the medium's mind. They could send their appearance or even show the home where they lived when they were alive. The medium will then describe whatever the spirit is visually showing them. It's amazing what spirits can send, and it's our job to just give what we are receiving — the more detailed, the better.

I never know what a spirit will show me, but they definitely do know what to send when they want to get a message across. There have been numerous times during a reading when a spirit has gotten me to arch my back and look upward toward the ceiling. To me, this always means that the spirit is trying to show me that they or the recipient of the message has a tie to the Sistine Chapel in Italy. I'll see Michelangelo's beautiful painting that adorns the chapel ceiling and it's as though I'm seeing it through the eyes of the spirit. With practice and experience the images that the Spirit World will send you will generally have the same meaning to you in all your readings.

Exercise: Opening Your
Psychic Sense of Clairvoyance

The following exercise should help you to understand where your psychic eye is located, and help you expand your inner vision.

Before you begin, get settled and relaxed in your own space. Turn off the computer and the phone. For this exercise, you'll need a small white votive candle.

Sit comfortably with the burning candle on a table in front of you. Relax your eyes and stare into the flame. You'll feel your eyes start to water, which is totally natural and to be expected. When they do, close your eyes and put the palms of each hand over each eye to create a total blackout.

You should now start to notice that the flame is flickering *inside* your mind's eye, slightly above and between your brows. Wait until the flame disappears, then repeat the exercise again for another 10 to 15 minutes. What you're actually doing in this exercise is training and developing your clairvoyant eye. (You'll find that this special spot is just above the bridge of your nose, not where you look straight out with your physical vision.)

The next time you want to use your psychic abilities to help answer a question or a decision, start by closing your eyes and gently focusing on your psychic eye, your third-eye chakra. Then go ahead and ask the question. As always, remember to be as specific as possible. When you're done, write down the original question in your journal along with the response, whether you saw a symbol, a word, a color, a person, or an object. By practicing and experimenting, you'll continue to sharpen this ability. Start off small with some simple tests. Try to guess the suit of playing cards by turning them upside down.

Additional Clairvoyance Exercises

I used to play the following simple game with my mother when I was a child. Little did I know that I was training my psychic abilities even at that young age! Have a friend think of a number from

1 to 50 and see if you can visualize it. Go with the first answer that pops into your psychic vision, rather than trying to think too hard. Let it be spontaneous.

Another great experiment is to have someone stand in another room and choose something to hold in their hands. From the other room where you're standing, keep a mental note of what you see, whether it's an image or an outline. Trust what you're receiving before your logical mind tries to shoot it down.

These exercises may seem simple, but what's actually happening is that you're beginning to stretch your abilities once again. Now you'll appreciate the saying: "Use it or lose it." You can make up your own experiments. There's so much more to see, once you learn to use this remarkable ability.

CLAIRAUDIENCE, OR "CLEAR HEARING"

Clairaudience is the inner sense of *hearing*. It's the ability to hear names, dates, certain sayings, and yes, even songs and melodies. Some people hear *objectively*, which is outside themselves. When you hear *subjectively* (in your mind), you'll become aware of sounds as though they're words spoken in your own voice.

Have you ever heard your name called out only to find out that no one was there? It may be from a loved one in Spirit, or it can be someone here who's thinking of you. If you feel it's the latter, try calling that person on the phone. Most likely, they'll tell you that they were just thinking of you.

Another good example of clairaudience is when you hear a song playing in your head. Not the song you just heard on the radio, but one that plays in your head unexpectedly and unwarranted. Stop for a minute and make a mental note of the song. What is the title? Listen to the words or try to find the lyrics on the Internet. It could be the favorite song of a loved one who has passed, and this is their way of saying hello. Most likely, there's a message of encouragement or advice for you within the words, or for someone close to you who needs a lift or a helping hand.

When I do a reading for someone over the phone, I use my ability of clairaudience by tuning into the energy via their voice. The voice is a powerful and expressive tool for picking up intuitive information. The next time you're on the phone with someone, close your eyes and really listen to their voice on the other end of the line. Let the person's tone and words completely enter your space so that your intuition takes over from your conscious reaction. You may notice colors, images, or even feelings that have nothing to do with the conversation. Don't just listen with your ears — listen with your intuition. Clairaudience is that small voice that you so often hear. You know, the one that so many of us don't listen to enough, only to regret it later.

This ability can be accessed through the throat reception area (throat chakra), and clairaudients can increase their psychic *listening strength* by focusing on this area.

Consider the following questions. Each *yes* is a strong indicator of clairaudience:

- Do you always think inside your head instead of out loud?

- Can you tell when someone's not telling the truth?

- Does a high-pitched sound ever suddenly come into your ear?

- Do you ever hear music or a particular song playing in your head?

- Do you ever hear what others are thinking?

Clairaudience can get a little confusing. How do you determine whether these are your own thoughts or psychic thoughts? After all, we have the tendency to talk to ourselves in our minds. The first stage of developing your clairaudient ability starts by learning to differentiate and separate psychic information from your everyday thoughts and mind chatter. To do this, you'll need to practice to improve your clairaudience. Over time, the information you receive, via your *inner voice* will start to flow and develop a sharper sense of clarity. Generally, this information should always be of the highest good and should have a positive feeling to it. If you're receiving negative information, then most likely there's some interference coming from your own mind. In this instance, you should consider checking to see if there are emotional or psychological issues that need to be addressed before you continue.

One very important piece of information I give to people who are beginning their psychic training is this: When you believe that you're receiving psychic information, step back and ask yourself: "Is this information coming *to* me or *from* me?" In doing so, you'll be able to maintain a balance with your psychic development and remain objective at all times.

Clairaudience on a Mediumship Level

When I started to study clairaudience, I always thought that I would hear a booming voice speak to me in crystal-clear words from the Spirit World. I thought I would hear objectively outside my head, not realizing that it's more common to hear subjectively inside your head, in your own voice. I know it's a spirit when I hear something that has nothing to do with my life.

On a mediumship level, when a medium is working with the rare ability of clairaudience, it can be quite specific and remarkable to witness. The medium's inner hearing is so acute and receptive that he or she may verbalize everything they're being told by the spirit. It's quite normal to hear a medium say names, nicknames, dates, addresses, numbers, and dates. Equally, if the spirit loved a certain type of music or a special song, the medium can hear the music played in their head. Of course, the medium's mind could filter what they're receiving. That's why I try to give off the information just like I'm hearing it.

A great story that proves this point is from when I was reading for a husband and wife who'd sadly lost their son. The session was going smoothly until I kept hearing the words *zipper head* in my head. I asked the parents if they understood that; they looked perplexed and said, "No, John. We don't understand that part."

Sometimes I'll be given the image of a zipper on a head clairvoyantly, and I know that's my frame of reference for a brain tumor. But this time, I kept hearing the words as opposed to seeing it as an image. I had to let it go because the young man had more to say, so I asked the parents to write down the zipper head reference in case it meant something later.

Shortly after this event, my office received a phone call from the parents telling us that they had an aha moment on the way home. Their son's nickname was Zip, and his computer log-in name was, in fact, Zipper Head!

As I've said, clairaudience can be hard to differentiate from your own thought, but with practice you will begin to know when it's Spirit talking. As you develop further, you'll be able to access your psychic hearing to assist you in many areas of your life. If clairaudience is your strength, then some of the following exercises might help you.

Exercise: Opening Your Psychic Sense of Clairaudience

Rather than getting comfortable in your own space at home, I want you to find a comfortable place outdoors, such as a park or the beach. Look for somewhere that people of all ages come together. Find a nice bench, a tree, or somewhere that feels comfortable.

Once you're settled, close your eyes, breathe in slowly, and relax. Take a few long deep breaths and just relax. Now try your hardest not to *look* but to *listen* with your physical hearing. Try to focus on the sounds from far off. See if you can hear the traffic, a plane, or voices of people talking. Reach out as far as you can with your hearing.

As you do this, try then bringing your hearing awareness closer to your surroundings. Can you hear the children playing? Can you hear other people speaking? Try to figure out the age difference in their voices. Are they young or old? Are there birds in the area? Notice all sounds far and near at the same time.

Now, while this is happening, try to listen to the silence in between the sounds. This is the special place where the undercurrent of intuitive information can often be heard.

This is probably one of the most challenging exercises, but what you're doing is training your physical hearing to reach different levels and ranges. I may use the word *hearing* but it's really more about *listening* to be able to receive impressions. An example of this is: When you are *hearing* a song, you are simply hearing the music and the lyrics being sung. But, when you are *listening* to a song, you are taking everything in, including the tempo, the words, and each instrument that is being played. There's a big difference between hearing and listening, so it's worth stopping for a moment to fully understand and appreciate the difference. In doing so, you'll actually sharpen your sense of clairaudience and become more familiar with that small voice within. Some people also find it helpful when developing clairaudience to put earplugs in their ears, to muffle some of the outside sounds. By turning down outside auditory influences, your inner hearing is accentuated and becomes more acute.

Additional Clairaudience Exercise

This is a good exercise to do toward the end of the day so you can let go of your thinking mind. Sit or lie down in a comfortable, quiet position. Take a deep breath and relax. Let the day slip away, close your eyes, and relax.

Now take a few moments to imagine a beautiful sky-blue light situated in your throat area. Imagine this light is slowly expanding as you breathe into this center. This is the center where clairaudience is accessed.

Ask any question that you'd like some guidance or clarity on, but as you're asking, remember to keep your awareness in this area as well as the sky-blue light. Don't be put off if at first you don't hear anything; eventually you may receive a word or even a sentence. Ask yourself whether the answer you received relates to the question you asked. If you don't understand the answer, ask yourself: "What does this mean to me?" More information could flow or it may be that your inner guidance wants to keep to the answer it originally gave. Trust what you're receiving, for you may notice at a later date that it was the perfect answer.

Once you become adept with this exercise, you can put it to good use at other times. For example, the next time you're about to go into a meeting, take a few moments, focus on your throat area, and ask: "What do I need to know for this meeting?" A word of advice may come to you, a song, or even a symbol that somehow seems to audibly speak to you in its own way. It can potentially influence your response and help achieve a better outcome from the meeting.

Remember that your angels, guides, and spirit helpers are also waiting to help you. All you have to do is ask and listen for their guidance. Use your journal to keep a record of what you're receiving and don't forget to date it, because you may receive information that won't initially make sense, but falls into place later in time.

————

Many of my students aspire to have clairaudience; if you're still developing, just go with what you have and any one of the three abilities (or a combination of them) will help you work mediumistically. Learn to play and have fun when developing your spiritual abilities. I can't teach you how to be psychic — because *you already are* — but I can help you remember it.

WEEKLONG CLAIR CHALLENGE: SURRENDER

I wrote earlier that being psychic is a way of being. Making time for activities that contribute to your spiritual growth and psychic development is not a sign of selfishness; by doing so, it can have a major impact on your overall well-being and spiritual vitality. Spending time to focus on your soul's needs enables you to nurture yourself and expand your spiritual boundaries. Therefore, for just one week I encourage you to do things that are uncharacteristic for you. In other words: things that you wouldn't normally do.

During this test week, surrender and trust your intuitive psychic abilities completely.

- If you *feel* that you've always wanted to have lunch with someone at work but never made the effort, then make this week the time to ask.

- If you *feel* drawn to call a relative who you've not spoke to in a long time — call.

- If there's a road that you've always wanted to drive down on your way home from work but never did, then drive down that road!

- Is there a book that you've always wanted to read, or one that you were drawn to even though it's not really a subject or story line that you usually are interested in? Get it.

- If you are continually drawn to a certain class or workshop, then at least inquire about it.

You know what I'm trying to say. I want you to trust and follow your gut, use all your psychic senses. After doing this for one week, don't forget to journal any new discoveries or revelations that resulted by following your inner guidance. Sometimes when you follow the prompting of your soul, it could easily lead to other opportunities. This amazing exercise will teach you how the flow of intuitive or psychic information runs through you and works for you. What I'm trying to do here is to get you to live intuitively and less analytically. Go for it!

As you learn to reawaken and develop your individual psychic ability, whether it's clairsentience, clairvoyance, or clairaudience, please remember to stay grounded and balanced. When these abilities are properly developed, they can greatly assist you in all areas of your life, including your spiritual development. Most important, it should be a wonderful experience and journey as you discover and build up your psychic senses.

Flex those intuitive muscles! The more you use them, the stronger they'll get.

PSYCHOMETRY: THE PSYCHIC TOUCH

The word *psychometry* was continuously used throughout my training (both in the U.S. and in the U.K.). It quickly became part of my teachings, and I recommend that all my students study and experiment with this wonderful training tool. The word means "measure of the soul."

Psychometry is an excellent and fun tool for you to use as you develop your psychic awareness. This little technique has some great benefits that will help you reach out beyond your five physical senses, by silencing or quieting your conscious mind to reach a psychic level. When you practice with psychometry, you'll be using one or more of your psychic strengths, whether it's clairsentience, clairvoyance, or clairaudience.

This is the practice of holding someone's personal possession and then *reading* the object as part of a psychic reading. To put it into a broader context, it's when you use your psychic ability to *sense* or experience the nature and history of the object or article. It's as if you're somehow *feeling, seeing,* or *hearing* through touch and receiving impressions. It's possible to deduce information about people or events associated with them solely by touching an object. Remember that everything is made up of energy and has its own auric emanations. It could be your favorite ring, a watch, the shirt you're wearing, or even that old chair you love to sit in.

When students try this technique for the first time, it's amazing to watch and hear what they receive from the object they're holding, but when I ask them to tell me what they received, I'm listening to their words, to see if they say: "I *saw* this, I *felt* that, or I *heard* . . ." I'm accessing what strength they're using. Sometimes it could be just one, but more often all three abilities will work together in unison.

I have a friend who uses this every time she gets a new contract. When she gets a business card from someone and that business card most likely has the owner's energy on it, she can get impressions from it. She stops and holds the card, tunes in to ask herself how she's feeling — positive or negative — and this helps her make the right business decision.

Try it for yourself the next time you pick something up. Think about the object you're holding and ask yourself whether it feels positive or negative. For example, have you ever borrowed someone's shirt or sweater and it made you feel different? What's happening is that you're picking up that person's emotions and their essence. Just a helpful hint based on my past experience: I've found that metal items seem to work even better. Watches, necklaces, rings, and keys seem to hold on to the owner's energy even stronger. The longer the item has been worn or in the person's possession the better.

I've also worked with flowers. By holding a flower that someone else has held, you can feel the energy that passed between the two living things. Flower clairsentience was first introduced to me while I was attending the Arthur Findlay College in the U.K. All the flowers were arranged in a vase, and no one in the class had any idea who had brought which flower. There were so many different shapes, sizes, and colors. We then chose the one that we were attracted to the most. By holding the flower, we used psychometry and read for the person who had brought it to establish a strong link — often with someone in Spirit too. It was as if holding a beautiful rose was a way to open the door into another world.

Psychometry can lay a good foundation for psychic work, and I highly recommend it if you're looking to develop your abilities.

Exercise: Psychometry

Before beginning this exercise, be sure to work through the previous exercises in this book. By now, you should have established one or more of your psychic strengths, whether it's clairsentience, clairvoyance, or clairaudience.

This simple exercise starts by holding something that belongs to someone else, something that has special meaning to them. You'll be trying to keep your thoughts out of it, so you remain totally objective. (For this reason, it would be better if you don't know very much about the person whose item you'll be holding.)

While you hold the object, focus on the appropriate chakra associated with the psychic ability you are using. Putting your awareness on the proper chakra will enhance your psychic strength. (As a reminder: clairsentience = solar plexus, clairaudience = throat, clairvoyance = third-eye.)

You don't need to grip the object tightly; just hold it lightly in your dominant hand. Keep turning it around in your hand as the images and feelings begin to form. If you can, write down the first few things that come to mind, but *don't* analyze or give your conscious mind a chance to shoot down what you're receiving.

Ask questions in your mind while you're holding the object, such as:

- Is this person married?
- Do they have children?
- Are they happy?
- What do they do for work?
- Can this person handle the job that I'm about to offer them?
- What advice can I give to help them right now?

The list of questions is endless. Share what you've received, whether it's feelings, words, images, or symbols, with the owner of the object. You might be amazed with how the information you receive translates into fact.

Once you become proficient with psychometry and there is a potential for mediumship, you'll be able to use it as a valuable tool to establish a link with the Other-Side. It's almost as if by using your psychic strengths combined with psychometry, you're tuning yourself to a higher frequency to connect with the spiritual realms and beings. Over time and with practice, you'll understand and be able to easily differentiate between what you're receiving psychically as opposed to mediumistically. Remember, they are different.

Just to recap: Psychics *perceive* information from a person's aura or from items they're holding that belong to the person they're reading, whereas mediums *receive* information from the Spirit World.

So, if someone gives you an item that belonged to a loved one who has passed and you feel you're beginning to get a connection from a spirit, before you go on, try putting the ring down. The reason that you should do this is to make sure you are *not* working on a psychic link. Someone who is not educated in the workings of spirit communication may think the information is coming from a spirit when, in fact, they are still picking up the psychic emanations from the item. If after putting the item down you still receive evidence and validation of a spirit, then you will know you are working on a mediumship level rather than a psychic level.

Enjoy practicing, and remember to get out of your own way and not to overanalyze everything you are receiving. Once again, journal everything!

Chapter 9

THE HUMAN PSYCHIC ATMOSPHERE

I step onstage and look out at the sea of expectant faces, all eager to hear what I'm about to say or the messages from Spirit. They sit there anxiously waiting for me to start, hoping they'll be the lucky recipients of a message from their loved ones.

I've often wondered if people are curious about what the medium is experiencing when they walk out to an awaiting audience or how it works? I'm sure that each and every one of us has our own ritual and routine. Of course, I have my own. Before I go onstage for a public demonstration or a private, one-on-one sitting, I clear my mind and get out of the way. Once I do that, my aura is open and I am open and ready to receive messages from Spirit. As I've been doing this work long enough now, I don't have to practice any extraordinary or specific techniques to open my aura; by thinking of the Spirit World and saying a prayer, it happens quite naturally. I just aim my thoughts — like a beam of light — to the Spirit World and let them know that I'm ready to work and to be of service to them, as well as their loved ones here.

Most people may not realize that the communication they're about to witness doesn't come *from* me, but *through* me. Often, as I start my introduction, I start to *feel* the Spirit People draw close to me as my aura begins to register their presence. Then the appropriate chakra activates and responds by enabling my clairsentience, clairvoyance, or clairaudience to discern the messages being sent from Spirit. Once this happens, the bridge between the two realms has been built and the reunion has begun!

When it comes to the development of your psychic or mediumship potential, your aura and chakras play a vital role. That is why the next two chapters are dedicated to the aura and chakras, and how they can assist us in reaching that greater part of ourselves.

The aura and chakras work together in partnership. The aura receives spiritual and psychic energy, and it's the means by which your chakras are fed. Your psychic strengths, aura, and chakras are all part of the mechanics used to enhance your natural psychic ability, as well as to develop your mediumship potential, which will enable you to connect to the Spirit World.

It's worth reiterating here that while Part II of this book was written to aid the development of your spiritual abilities, even those who choose not to become a psychic or medium will also benefit. Gaining a deeper understanding of your inner self will assist you not just with your spiritual life, but also with your physical life.

WHAT IS AN AURA?

As we progress through life, we're continually giving, receiving, and perceiving energy with everyone we come in contact with here in the physical world, as well as those on the Other-Side. Have you ever met someone for the first time and, out of nowhere, images and feelings just flood into your mind? It's times like these that you'll immediately know whether you're going to like this person. It's often a really strong feeling. Equally, you may form a picture of their life in your mind or have a sense of what they do for a living. You may even pick up whether they're married or single and so much more. In that split second, during that *first* introduction, you'll get a total download of all sorts of information, as your mind begins to decipher and interpret what you're receiving. What's really going on at this moment is that you're actually reading and interpreting their *aura*.

Here's another scenario. Have you ever experienced *feeling* the presence of a loved one who has passed, or had a thought of them suddenly come into your mind? Even though they're in the spiritual realm, their spiritual body has an aura, which lovingly reaches out to yours.

We've all seen religious paintings of saints and angels, often depicted with golden halos around their heads. These images represent the spiritual light of the aura. But you don't have to be a saint or an angel to possess an aura. Each and every one of us has our own unique aura. Over the years, auras have been described in a number of diverse ways. But to put it as simply as possible, it's the energy field that surrounds *all* matter. The human aura, which surrounds the body, emanates in all directions, and it's usually oval in shape, manifesting itself as a magnetic field. This energy constantly flows and changes according to our mood. It adapts to our emotional, mental, and physical states. Even our personal history gets documented and recorded in our aura, such as our memories, ideas, goals, and physical ailments, as well as who we really are! No medical record could ever contain this much information.

There are many layers to the aura, and it's only a trained clairvoyant's eye that's able to see all the layers. The *etheric* layer is the closest to the body, followed by the *astral* layer, the *mental* layer, and finally the *spiritual* layer. The more psychically sensitive you are, the more you'll be able to see and feel the layers within the human energy field. It's a fact that we *all* sense auras of both people and places, but few of us ever realize that it's happening.

The following situations are all examples of experiencing an aura:

- Being in line at a bank or post office and *knowing* when someone stepped behind you before you turned around.

- Feeling someone staring at you from across a room.

- Feeling naturally drawn to certain colors.

- Noticing when you feel comfortable or uncomfortable in certain rooms.

- Feeling comfortable around some people, while others leave you feeling drained.

- Feeling the presence of a passed loved one standing right beside you.

I believe that our prehistoric ancestors, such as primitive man, relied on their auras to feel, sense, and detect when danger was impending. After all, they had no other detection system, so they had to rely on their own senses and abilities to make that judgment call, whether they were alerted to a friend or a foe. Over time, we've gradually lost some of this raw sensory ability, but it's possible to learn how to reawaken and use it again.

The intensity of color and the brightness of the aura may reveal the status of a person's health, as well as their mental and emotional state. Every aura is unique and vibrates to its own distinct frequency. It's possible that with practice, you'll be able to increase your auric vibration so you can expand it out or draw it in closer to you. When your aura is open and you're vibrating at the same frequency with someone or something else, even a physical place, that's often the time when you'll sense a *connection*. Similarly, when other people don't resonate with you, it's usually because they're vibrating at a different frequency. This is why you may feel a sense of *disconnection*, or what I like to refer to as *bumping auras*. Of course, there'll be times when it takes longer to blend with someone else's energy before both of you will feel comfortable with each other.

Now let's move on to seeing and sensing the aura for yourself. People who have the ability of clairvoyance will see the aura, whereas clairaudients will hear certain words emanate from the aura, and clairsentients will feel or sense the aura. No matter what psychic sense is strongest, *everyone* can discover the best way to understand and read an aura.

Example of an aura

DEVELOPING AURIC VISION

I believe that some people are *attracted* to light, while others *emanate* it. I had an incredible experience that validates this when I was demonstrating at the Omega Institute in Rhinebeck, New York.

I'd just stepped onstage to give a demonstration of mediumship to an eagerly awaiting audience. I kicked off the demonstration with my usual explanation of how I work as a spirit messenger. I was explaining about the quickening process, where I raise my vibrations and spirits lower theirs as we blend. Even before I'd finished explaining about this delicate process, I was suddenly very drawn to a woman in the middle of the audience. I couldn't take my eyes off her!

Now it's important to stress here that when I give out messages, I really have no idea to whom I will be drawn, what the connection with the audience member will be, or the nature of the message. But this woman seemed to be glowing, as if from the inside out. It was an extraordinary sight, and I was conscious that I was witnessing something quite unique. The rest of the audience seemed to fade around her as I observed a luminous and dazzling light emanating from all around her. Her aura was literally beaming! To this day, I have never seen one so beautifully illuminated.

It turned out her name was Elizabeth, and I quickly established that her husband had passed away some years before. He was a gentle spirit, and his love was evident in his beautiful message for her that night, which flowed easily and effortlessly as she sat there, smiling and nodding her head to confirm all his information.

Elizabeth had enrolled in the workshop that I was teaching that weekend, hoping to hear from her husband. Well, she certainly got her wish. I knew that he was standing right beside her and that his energy and love had somehow amplified her auric light. Later that evening, other people who had been sitting near Elizabeth expressed how they'd felt a tingling sensation. It was obvious that they'd blended with her aura and felt the spiritual emanations of this lovely woman and the love of her husband.

One of the most popular segments I teach in my workshops is how to see auras. Now I don't want to mislead you into thinking that you're going to wake up one day and start seeing these energy fields as a matter of course. Equally, you can't just read a book and suddenly be able to see them. However, once you realize that you're not necessarily viewing auras with your physical eyes but with your *psychic inner eye*, then you'll have a better understanding of how to see the auric light that surrounds everyone and everything. I find it helpful to imagine yourself as a being of light and energy because, in reality, you are!

Exercise: Seeing the Auric Light

To increase your chances of viewing an aura, I suggest that for this exercise you find a dimly lit room with as little direct sunlight as possible. You may be able to use your special place if the lighting is adjustable. You'll also need a blank wall for a volunteer to stand in front of, which should preferably be a neutral color and free from pictures or ornaments. When viewing someone's aura, it's best to have your volunteer wear pale, light-colored clothes. I know that sounds like a lot of conditions, but it's worth getting the stage set right to enable this to work properly.

Begin by closing your eyes and taking a few deep breaths. Once you're relaxed, bring your awareness up to your third eye. I believe that the aura is a type of "viewing screen" for your third eye, and with practice you'll be able to strengthen your vision to see auras all the time. As you open your physical eyes, keep your awareness on the point between your brows. (This doesn't mean that you should roll your eyes up into your head!) Take your time here.

When you feel you're ready, have your friend sit or stand in front of the blank wall. Position yourself far enough away so that you can see their entire body. Remember that you're looking at them with your psychic eye, so keep your awareness between your brows. Start by looking at the space just to the side of your friend's head and shoulders, so it's like you're looking past them.

They should only be in your peripheral vision — don't struggle to focus on them.

Allow your eyes to relax as you continue to look at the space *beside* your friend. Now, by using your breath, continue to hold your awareness in your third-eye chakra and ask your friend to slowly rock back and forth. You should begin to notice a whitish-blue glow form around their head and shoulder area, which should mirror their rocking movement.

This whitish glow will be the first thing most people see. When you become more sensitive and trained, you may begin to see various hues of color.

Try to observe if the aura is larger in one area than another, or whether there are hints of various colors around it. Many psychic impressions can be seen and felt in the aura, so at this point it's important to let any intuitive information flow freely.

To finish this exercise, close your eyes, take a breath, and bring your awareness back down to your physical eyes. Take a moment to relax and breathe. If you want to, try switching places to let your friend see your aura. When you're finished, try to write down the experiences in your journal. If you feel comfortable talking at the same time, try telling your friend what you see so that they can give you their feedback.

Just to repeat, you're not going to wake up one day and immediately be able to see auras. If you don't see anything right away, that's okay — you're learning a new way of seeing, so take your time and don't give up. When I first started, it took me some time to get it right. Keep practicing this exercise. Once you see your first aura, you'll suddenly start noticing them all the time with less and less effort. In time, you'll be able to expand your auric vision to see more levels, and the colors will intensify, becoming more vibrant and more visible.

And don't limit your practice to people. Try to see the auras of plants and trees when you're outside. I remember one particularly cloudless day, when I saw the aura of a pine tree for the first time against the deep-blue sky. I stood there for several minutes, totally transfixed. It created a visual memory that I've never forgotten.

SENSING THE AURA

Auras *really do* exist, even if you cannot initially see them! It may be that you're more clairsentient, and will have a stronger ability to sense rather than see an aura. You may have seen healers working on someone's aura as they move their hands over the body, smoothing, rebalancing, and healing the person's energy field. The hands are wonderful receptors of energy and it's possible to obtain psychic insights and impressions this way.

As I've explained, the aura extends far beyond your physical body. So now you'll start to notice those times when you approach a place or a situation that doesn't feel right to you. You'll become more aware when you're at a social or business gathering and you find yourself drawn to a certain person or, equally, when you feel you need to distance yourself from someone. When you find yourself in these situations, stop and observe how you're feeling, what you're sensing, even what colors you're perceiving. By doing so, you're giving your inner guidance a chance to give you some psychic insights that may be quite useful in that situation.

You can learn to *expand* your aura, and there are many reasons why you would want to do this, whether you're about to do a psychic reading, going to a concert and want to feel and experience the richness of the music, or even if you're off outdoors and you just want to heighten the whole experience with nature. We're all made up of energy, so you can blend your aura with another person, spirit, a plant, or even your trusted pet. Also, it's very important to know and remember that you can also learn to *contract* (to draw in) your aura if you want to be less sensitive to your physical surroundings, or psychic and mediumistic emanations. By doing this, you're striving to be the master of your abilities and not let them become the master of you. You can pull back, recharge, and expand your aura in a number of ways, by using the power of the breath, meditation, and bringing color into your aura by simply using the ability of your imagination and thought. The advantages and benefits of knowing you're in control of your aura are limitless.

In the next two exercises, we're going to learn how to *feel* the auric energy surrounding the human body.

Exercise: Feeling the Energy

As always, get yourself comfortable; take a seat or stand in a comfortable position. Take in a deep cleansing breath, let it out, and relax. Just breathe in and let it out once again.

Now rub the palms of your hands together briskly for about 20 to 30 seconds. This will make your hands even more sensitive and receptive. Place your palms slightly in front of you (about 12 inches) so they're facing each other. Slowly bring your palms together, pull them apart again, then back together. Don't let the palms touch. Keep the distance to about 12 inches each time as you pull them apart.

You should begin to notice a slight pressure (like two magnets repelling each other) developing between your hands. You may also feel a slight temperature change or a tingling sensation. This is quite normal. You can even create what is known as an "energy ball," which is simply a ball of energy that builds up between your hands. Other people close to you may also feel this energy, especially if they run the palms of their hands slowly between yours.

This is a great exercise! This exercise will assist you in feeling your energy field. With continued practice, your hands will become highly tuned receptors for those subtle vibrations.

As always, I encourage you to document your experiences and observations in your journal.

Exercise: Tuning into the Aura

This exercise takes what you learned in the previous exercise one step further. I'm going to show you how to sense someone's aura and pick up some psychic sensations and impressions. This exercise requires two people working together, so you'll need your trusted friend again and a comfortable low-back chair.

Decide between the two of you who's going to be the "sitter" and who will be the "feeler." The sitter then takes a seat with their feet flat on the floor and their palms facing upward on their lap. Once you're in position, take a nice deep breath and relax. The feeler should be standing just behind the chair, with a straight yet relaxed posture. Take another nice slow breath. The feeler should now rub their palms together as we did in the previous exercise for about 15 seconds.

Now the sitter should start thinking about a situation in their life that was unpleasant. Please let the sitter know that they won't have to hold that thought long, as it's just a memory. The feeler should place their palms about 10 inches away from the sitter's head and *slowly* move their hands around that area without touching it. Then the feeler's hands should move down to the sitter's shoulder area. The feeler should slowly pull their palms out and back in again. It's important to concentrate, so if you're the feeler, you notice where the aura starts and how far it extends.

You should start to notice the sensation in your hands at this point. See if you can *feel* whether the sitter's aura has expanded or is still tight around them. Can you notice any temperature changes and if so, where are you noticing them? Are there any colors you can sense or feel? Keep a mental note of everything so you can explain it all afterward.

Now the feeler should hold their hands in one position (preferably a few inches above the sitter's head). Close your eyes and focus on your third-eye area and see if you can pick up clairvoyantly what the sitter's putting out. Are you seeing any images, symbols, or colors? Remember what you received. The sitter can now *release* that unpleasant thought (it's just a memory from the past) and at the same time surround it with a healing white light, while the feeler should shake their hands toward the floor, away from themselves and the sitter.

The energy will be absorbed and cleansed by the earth. Don't give off the information that you received just yet.

Now it's time to change directions. This time the sitter should think of one of the happiest days in their life. Repeat the process as above. The feeler should rub their palms together again and begin to feel the aura around the sitter's head and shoulder area. Notice if there are any changes. Is the aura contracted or expanded this time? Is the temperature different? Have the colors changed? Are your hands feeling more sensitive with that tingling sensation? Now, with your hands in one position again, see if you can feel any impressions about the sitter's happiest day. Finally, shake off the energy from your hands and share all the information you've gathered with the sitter.

Feedback is essential when developing your psychic sensitivity to see if you're on track. I suggest you experiment by switching places and give the sitter a chance to feel and understand the aura if they wish. Please remember everyone's aura is different, and this is a great way of increasing your psychic sensitivity as well as your confidence in feeling and interpreting auras without even seeing one.

Exercise: Aura in Mediumship Training

Once you're proficient in feeling your own and others' auras, and you feel ready to use your aura to reach out to the Spirit World, then this exercise is great for beginning to explore that realm.

You will need a sitter, preferably someone whose relatives you're not familiar with. Arrange two chairs facing each other, and have the sitter get comfortable before you start. Explain that you're going to read their aura and try to link and blend with someone that they've lost to a passing. I encourage you to write down your impressions as you practice. (A benefit of having a notepad is that it often helps your sitter feel less nervous, as you're not staring at them!)

Begin by bringing in the white light of the Universe and let it enter your heart area. Take your time and just breathe it into your heart. Let this beautiful light fill your heart and then let it slowly fill you, as if your entire being is being illuminated. Imagine this light expanding beyond your body and encompassing the person in front of you. It's almost as if the two of you are in some sort of invisible bubble together. The goal here is to reach out with your aura and blend with the aura of the person in front of you.

Psychics work this way to assist the person they are working with in obtaining their greatest need. Open your mind and *see*, *feel*, or *hear* (depending on your psychic strength) if there are any impressions you're receiving from their aura. It could be a color, an image, a scene, a word, or a situation that's taking place in their life. Write down everything you're receiving. I find it helpful to look over one of their shoulders so their aura becomes a viewing screen. The sitter shouldn't be trying to send you any information; it's your job to read them. Be open and keep writing down what you're receiving. As always, don't overanalyze the information you're receiving.

Now let's step it up bit. Don't focus your awareness on the person in front of you, but aim your awareness using your mind and try to reach out to the Spirit People who may be connected to the sitter. Set the intention to the Spirit World and your guides that you would like someone to come forward — someone this person knows and can validate. Take your time. You may begin to feel, see, or hear a spirit. Mediumship doesn't need to be overly dramatic. You may receive something subtle. In the beginning, you might just sense the spirit's gender. If you forge a good link and feel a connection, then ask the spirit whether they're young or old, then try to ascertain how they passed. You might feel a sensation in your own body. Whatever you're experiencing, relay the exact information to the person you're sitting with, without putting your own interpretation on it. Just give what you're receiving and try not to question it, while asking the sitter to validate and endorse the information. This is part of the authentication process of confirming the identity of the spirit.

Remember to keep your awareness focused on the Spirit World as opposed to the sitter. Ask them gently to come closer to blend with you even more. Remember this is not possession — just linking and blending as the spirit overshadows your own spiritual body with their aura. Also, a great tip (whether you're working with a single person or an audience) is to try to remember to also have a light awareness on the individual chakra that's associated with your unique ability. I find that this helps to tune in (much like a radio signal) to information being sent from the Spirit World. But have no worries; as I've said previously, when doing mediumship, the Spirit People will most likely try to use all three of your "clair" abilities. Of course, the strongest ability will always be more prominent.

If you're starting out and learning the mechanics, I recommend you try this for just a few minutes at a time, until you become more familiar with the whole process and the sensations that come with it. It's most important to thank the spirit for coming through as they step back, as you slowly pull back your energy (aura) so that it's completely back with you and your physical body. And always remember to close down your chakras. (I'll be sharing an exercise describing how to do so in the next chapter.) The connection is now closed and you're completely here and grounded in the physical world.

If the potential is there, you'll slowly become more proficient with your mediumship. If you feel you're not receiving anything from the Spirit World, then it could mean that you still need to become more sensitive before you can be receptive to the spiritual realms. I'd rather you take your time and have a solid psychic foundation and education before you move on to exploring your mediumship abilities. It took me several years of doing psychic work before the Other-Side showed up! Once they started to make their presence known, I had another two years of training and studying the intricate mechanics of this work. You can't rush or force your spiritual abilities because if you try, it could impede your natural growth and affect you physically, emotionally, and mentally. I'll always say, "Patience, my friend. Patience."

STRENGTHENING & CLEANSING YOUR AURA

A strong, well-balanced, and cleansed aura is *essential* to everyone, both on a physical and spiritual level. It's important for you to learn and understand everything you can about this special energy source. You should consciously strive to achieve a powerful auric field.

We're constantly bombarded by external influences. The aura can be affected by the state of your mind and body, as well as your emotions, the people around you, and your immediate environment. If your aura becomes weak, you can end up feeling tired, drained, or, in the most severe cases, powerless to make choices or decisions. If this continues, physical symptoms will become noticeable. Health problems can occur as well as mental and emotional imbalances. In these cases, as always, seek out the advice of your doctor.

Your aura is a wonderful early detection system. It will alert you to a problem early on, so you have time to do something about it. When it's healthy and strong, it acts as a protective shield. Your aura can be strengthened in a number of different ways. It doesn't require a lot of work and can help you stay healthy, improve your psychic and mediumistic abilities, keep you safe, and help you attract *only* what's best for you.

Many therapists and mediums, including myself, use Himalayan salt baths as a means to cleanse their auras. If you think about it, we originated from the ocean, and many of us through our lives are constantly drawn back to it. We find ourselves forever seeking out the nearest ocean. How often have you come back from a day at the beach feeling totally relaxed and invigorated? It's not just the sun or the sound of those crashing waves that are responsible, it's the salt from the ocean and the air, which ionizes your aura, thereby cleansing and strengthening it. You're refreshed, as though your problems have been washed away. No wonder bath salts are such a hit!

It should go without saying that regular physical exercise and being outdoors in the sunshine, breathing in fresh air — rich in oxygen and prana — will help strengthen and revitalize your aura. If you work in an air-conditioned office with artificial lights, make a big effort to go out for a short walk at lunchtime, even if it's for just 10 minutes.

I strongly advocate that everyone complement what nature provides through different healing practices, such as massage, Reiki, therapeutic touch, polarity, aromatherapy, and acupuncture. Any of these natural treatments will greatly reinforce and replenish your energy field. As always, you should find what works and feels the best for you.

Diet and a healthy lifestyle play a big part in keeping your aura balanced; as I constantly preach, do everything in moderation. Too much alcohol, tobacco, or those dreaded fast foods will all have a negative effect on your aura and will weaken your energy system.

Just being *aware* of your aura is a great start. You get dressed every morning to protect yourself from the elements, right? Well this is a perfect time to place a protective thought on your aura. Do this before you start your busy day, so you can not only attract positivity, but also repel negativity, whether it's from a person or a place. See your aura as a brilliant white light that acts as an invisible shield that surrounds and stays with you throughout the day. Take time to rest and relax as much as possible, and, of course, every time you meditate you'll be building your psychic strength, as well as expanding and reinforcing your precious aura.

Chapter 10

WHEELS OF LIGHT

As humans, we're continually seeking out different places to find enlightenment, whether at a church, a synagogue, or any one of the many sacred locations all over the world. As we persistently search within for our own spirit, we have a tendency to look outside ourselves for direction and guidance, and even the answers. (I should stress here that I certainly don't undervalue the importance many people put on places of worship, as I often visit churches myself for the wisdom, peace, and solitude contained therein, which comforts and uplifts me.) However, when we begin to understand and work with our chakra system, we soon come to realize and appreciate that our bodies are truly our temples.

When I think of chakras, I imagine them as beautiful spinning wheels of spiritual light. I remember the first time I heard the word *chakra*. I was intrigued by every aspect of it, from the sound itself to its origins and meaning. Then and there, I made a promise to myself that I'd dedicate as much time and energy as necessary to learn what this fascinating word truly meant. Of course, I didn't realize at the time what an important function chakras have to the development of our spiritual abilities as well as our overall well-being. I like to call these seven main centers "spiritual batteries" because of the vital energy that runs through them, and I'm aware just how important they are and the role they play in your psychic equipment — which is you!

WHAT ARE CHAKRAS?

There are seven major chakras (as well as many minor ones) that play an important function in your physical and spiritual life, and each corresponds to an endocrine gland in your body. During the early stages of your psychic development, I suggest that you focus on these seven main centers.

The chakras run upward along the spinal cord. Energy enters from both the front and back of each one. Chakras are the link between your *physical body* and your *aura*, and they constantly interact with one another. Each one is complemented by a distinctive auric color and has its own unique function. The seven centers act as sensitive contact points, or bridges, where the physical and spiritual worlds meet. The lower chakras deal with the physical body and relate to all the issues associated with living in the material world, such as survival, health, careers, safety, and the home. The upper or higher chakras deal with all psychic and spiritual abilities.

Your actions and thoughts play a big part in controlling this flow of energy, as well as the functions of the chakras. Even though the energy that runs through these centers remains constant, it can be increased or decreased, depending on how well you balance your life. For instance, if you're worrying about money matters (earthly, *physical* concerns), then your *lower* chakras are likely to be affected in a negative way, slowing down their *rate* and *spin*. When this happens the disbursement of energy will be weaker, and as a result you may feel sluggish or out of balance.

In contrast, when you're feeling compassionate toward someone, or if you're focusing on higher spiritual thoughts, then the *upper* chakras are more prone to spin freely, resulting in the energy being dispersed freely, which creates a feeling of harmony and vitality. There has to be *balance* when you activate and work with your chakras. You should never focus on stimulating just one at any given time, as all seven of them should be in balance so that the flow of energy can travel through them evenly to the appropriate areas.

I believe that you're meant to have unlimited amounts of energy and should be able to tap into your creative talents easily, as well as live a life of love, compassion, and, most important, a life of peace. It's possible to gain powerful guidance for your life once you turn inward and consult your inner wisdom. By allowing the natural balance of energies to flow through your spiritual batteries — where transformation truly begins — you'll be able to *hear*, *see*, and *feel* the voice of your higher self, as well as those in the Spirit World, with greater clarity.

THE SEVEN ENERGY CENTERS

Every chakra has a set of related colors, sounds, and glands, as well as key words that will make it resonate. Understanding and learning these reference points will enhance and support a greater physical and spiritual understanding.

Let's look at all seven chakras.

Chakra	Color	Sound	Gland
Base (root)	Red	Lam	Adrenals
Sacral	Orange	Vam	Testicles, ovaries
Solar plexus	Yellow	Ram	Pancreas, adrenals
Heart	Green	Yam	Thymus
Throat	Light blue	Ham	Thyroid
Third eye	Indigo	Om	Pituitary
Crown	Violet	Silence	Pineal

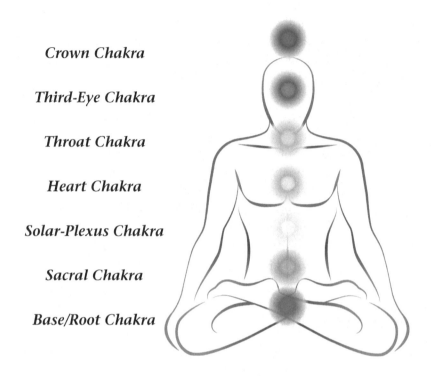

Crown Chakra

Third-Eye Chakra

Throat Chakra

Heart Chakra

Solar-Plexus Chakra

Sacral Chakra

Base/Root Chakra

1. The Base or Root Chakra

- *Color:* Red
- *Sound:* Lam
- *Gland:* Adrenals

Situated at the base of the spine, the base or root chakra is most closely related to all earthly issues, such as survival, the physical body, and financial concerns, as well as sustenance, safety, and shelter. This is the center where we draw in energy to support us.

When the energy of this chakra is blocked, or depleted, you may have a sense of not feeling totally grounded. This could cause you to say, "I don't feel quite right today" or "I'm just not feeling myself." You may also experience fatigue, feel lethargic or unmotivated, be prone to seek approval, or be overly cautious.

An overactive first chakra, on the other hand, may cause you to suffer from anger or feel unduly aggressive, impulsive, hyperactive, or even reckless.

To balance this chakra, yoga is highly beneficial, as well as dancing or light physical exercise, such as tai chi, which will assist in keeping the energy flowing and balanced.

If you're feeling slightly spacey, try imagining roots spreading from the base of your spine and digging themselves into the earth like a tree. I know this sounds a little crazy, but this simple thought process will enable you to remain grounded in the present. Finally, keep in mind that honoring your body and taking care of it on the *outside* will benefit you *inside*. It works both ways!

2. The Sacral Chakra

- *Color:* Orange

- *Sound:* Vam

- *Gland:* Testicles, ovaries

Located two fingers below the navel, the sacral chakra relates to emotions, desires, creativity, and sexuality.

An underactive sacral chakra can cause you to experience a lower sexual drive, or you may become introverted, or even worry about what others think of you. When it becomes overactive, then you can feel sexually aggressive, jealous, or possessive, or you may suffer from lower back pain or kidney problems.

When your sacral chakra is balanced, you'll enjoy life and all it has to offer with passion and excitement. So, to keep the energy flowing, try different forms of dance in which you move your hips and your lower abdomen. To stimulate this chakra, use a color meditation, practice yoga, express your sexuality however you feel comfortable, and, above all, take time to nurture yourself. Remember, you *do* matter!

3. The Solar-Plexus Chakra

- *Color:* Yellow
- *Sound:* Ram
- *Gland:* Pancreas, adrenals

Located between the navel area and the rib cage, the solar-plexus chakra represents power, vitality, self-control, self-esteem, and confidence. This is the center where all your emotions and feelings are recorded; it's also associated with clairsentience, as it's a major psychic reception area.

When developing your psychic or mediumship abilities, you should be aware of this sensitive area and learn how to "close down" properly so that you avoid becoming too sensitive or receiving unwanted energies from people or certain places. (I'll be sharing an exercise on how to do so later in this chapter.)

When this chakra is properly balanced, you can come across as really confident, as though you're ready to take on the world. When it's unbalanced, you can become judgmental, have a tendency to plan things without following through, worry too much, or even suffer from nervous exhaustion. Stomach problems and digestive disorders, including ulcers, are common to this area when it's left unbalanced for too long.

To balance and open this chakra, you may want to consider energy healing work with a professional, or take some workshops and classes that focus on self-empowerment. It's also helpful to do breathwork complemented with color.

Final quick piece of advice: Be aware of people who *take* your energy.

4. The Heart Chakra

- *Color:* Green
- *Sound:* Yam
- *Gland:* Thymus

Found right where its name indicates, the heart chakra represents unconditional love, compassion, joy, balance, relationships, and healing. It's said to be the link between our mind, body, and Spirit. When I see a medium work with their heart center when they're delivering a message from the Spirit World, I can tell that the recipient of the message can really feel it. If it's in a larger crowd, *everyone* feels the love that's shared.

The chakra associated with the human heart is often filled with so much joy and happiness, as emotions flow so strongly through here that it's possible you'll find tears rolling down your face when you meditate. This is also the area where all past hurts, disappointments, and emotional scars reside, so as energy reaches this area, it will try to clear any blockages you may have. When the heart chakra is activated in the beginning stages of psychic or mediumship development, it's possible that you may experience moodiness or feel depressed. This is why I wrote earlier about taking care of yourself and being in a good emotional and mental state when developing your abilities.

By balancing the heart chakra, emotions that relate to past issues can be healed, which will then enable you to move on with your life. However, if left unbalanced, anger, jealousy, and heart conditions can potentially develop. An underactive heart chakra will cause you to experience self-worth issues, feelings of being unloved, or a lack of compassion.

Balancing this area may take a while, so be sure to take all the time you need for the healing energy to get through and flow freely to your other chakras. Loving yourself and others, performing acts of compassion, and learning to forgive, as well as being outdoors and surrounding yourself with the beauty of nature will all help to balance this area. A breath facilitator (a professional trained and certified in the art of *transformational breath*) and a therapist or counselor can assist you in working through blockages in your heart chakra to benefit your overall well-being and aid emotional healing.

5. The Throat Chakra

- *Color:* Light blue
- *Sound:* Ham
- *Gland:* Thyroid

Located, as you might expect, in the throat area, the throat chakra is associated with communication, sound, creativity, and the ability of clairaudience. Many artists, speakers, writers, singers, and other creative individuals often have highly attuned and active throat chakras.

Have you ever noticed someone who's constantly clearing their throat? When I observe this, I usually ask the person if they need to say something. People have a way of holding back what needs to be said, and in doing so, they can cause an "energy backup" in the throat area. Hence the saying, "They were choking on their words." When the throat chakra is unbalanced, it can lead to sore throats, skin irritations, and ear infections. As a result, tension creeps into the neck and shoulder areas. When it's underactive, you're likely to resist change, appear slow to respond, or become easily influenced by others.

By activating and balancing this center, you will be inspired to speak and listen to the truth, both for yourself as well as others. Try humming, chanting, or singing out loud, and, most important, if you have something to say, then please *speak up!* Once you've activated this chakra, don't be surprised if you suddenly become creatively inspired.

6. The Third-Eye Chakra

- *Color:* Indigo
- *Sound:* Om
- *Gland:* Pituitary

The third-eye chakra, which is the one that's most talked about, is associated with clairvoyance, intuition, and higher levels of consciousness. Found between the brows and just above the bridge of your nose, this chakra works closely with the throat and crown chakras to assist you with your psychic and intuitive inner guidance. Most psychics, artists, and people with vivid imaginations often have a well-developed third eye. With the proper development, you'll be able to "see" far beyond the limitations of ordinary sight and find solutions and choices that aren't necessarily right in front of you.

If this chakra stays underdeveloped, you could become afraid of success and unable to see the bigger picture, which is often a result of not being able to visualize yourself as happy and successful.

When this center is unbalanced, you could experience eyestrain, vision problems, undue worrying, headaches, or forgetfulness. I know that when I'm doing too much psychic work, I experience a band of tightness around my head, which is a sign that my third-eye chakra is overactive and I need to go to the gym or take a walk with my dog. It's time to bring the energy back down into my lower chakras for balance.

To balance the third-eye chakra, I recommend walking meditations, breathwork, and visualizations using color. But don't just focus on this one chakra as part of your development; it's important to remember that *all* the chakras must be in balance so that they can work in synchronized unison and harmony.

7. The Crown Chakra

- *Color:* Violet
- *Sound:* Silence
- *Gland:* Pineal

The crown chakra, located right at the top of the head, is also known as "The Thousand-Petaled Lotus" or "The Receiver of Light." It is the center of your link with the universe and your higher consciousness; in other words, it's the connection with wisdom and spiritual insight. The crown center is where spiritual light and energy are received and then dispersed throughout your aura for your total well-being.

When this chakra is stimulated and balanced, energy can flow up the spine and out through this center, like a beautiful fountain that washes over you with positive energy, elevating and enriching your spirit. By comparison, when left unbalanced, you can feel cut off, frustrated, depressed, or unhappy, and self-doubt can develop. You may even experience writer's block, which is when energy doesn't flow freely into the center, resulting in a lack of inspiration. However, when properly balanced, the crown chakra will expand to a point where it's possible to access and tap into the deepest sources of universal wisdom.

To balance this chakra, try meditation, breathwork, yoga, spiritual healing, acupuncture, and color visualizations.

CHAKRAS AND YOUR PSYCHIC ABILITIES

As you develop your psychic or mediumship abilities, becoming more proficient and experienced in using them, these centers will naturally open up more easily. If you're a beginner who is reading this book, I suggest studying and learning as much as you can about the chakra system. As they run up your spine, the chakras act like one big psychic antenna. Go slow when working with them, as they've always been with you, but you'll be activating them and using them more than you have in the past.

Your psychic ability is intrinsically linked to the chakras, so it's possible to stimulate your psychic centers purely by thought. However, too much psychic work or even talking about psychic matters can open you up and make you feel tired, moody, or even irritable. Keeping yourself cleansed and protected, and ensuring that you close down properly will become important practices in your personal development.

Don't forget that you're a *spiritual being* living in a *physical body*, and each deserves a 50:50 split of your time, energy, and devotion. That way you'll be able to stay grounded and balanced, so that your spirit and body can live and work together in harmony. Do remember that your inner guidance is just a part of you . . . it isn't *all* of you.

When you fully open your chakras, you'll expand your auric field at the same time. As I explained earlier, when this happens you'll become more susceptible to all the vibrations around you. Consequently, you'll begin to notice how sensitive you're becoming and you're likely to become more attuned to everyone and everything in your environment.

When I demonstrate onstage, I feel *everything*, including Spirit People on the Other-Side, people around me in the audience, and my own feelings. It's as though every sense is being bombarded, but at the same time charged with emotion. Fortunately for me, I've learned how to handle this influx of feelings, and I'm able to close down and manage the process. The nature of my work means that I'm often open and highly sensitive, so I find that too much time in big cities for prolonged periods (with all the noise, commotion, activity, and chaos) can often tip the scales into psychic overload.

So, I now live in the country, where the pace of life is slower, allowing the earth to ground me. I have time to meditate, exercise, and maintain a healthy and more balanced life. I know firsthand how important it is to take care of yourself when you're developing and operating your psychic equipment.

WORKING WITH YOUR CHAKRAS

In this last essential exercise, you'll be working with all seven major chakras. You'll imagine each of the seven centers as a small, colored, bright light. As you visualize these lights growing and shrinking in size, you'll be opening and closing your chakras. This practice will not only infuse your chakras with vitality and energy, but as with some of the other exercises, it will also heighten and expand your psychic awareness.

You'll start off with the base chakra and work your way up to the crown chakra. Keep in mind that the base chakra and crown chakras should always remain *open* and *balanced*, allowing you to be a conduit for precious life-giving energy to flow properly throughout your entire system, both physically as well as spiritually. Using the image of a colored light for each chakra, along with sending the thought to open and close each one, will often be enough to raise and amplify your psychic power.

This exercise is quite powerful, and there are a few important rules to follow:

1) Open your chakras in sequence;

2) Be aware of each chakra;

3) Close down each chakra properly.

Exercise: Raising the Power

Begin by sitting down in an upright position, with your spine straight and get comfortable. Take a few slow, complete breaths in and out as you relax.

Opening the chakras: Visualize a red light at the base of your spine. See the light begin to expand and grow in size. As it does, imagine that there's a brilliant white light coming up from the earth through the soles of your feet, up your legs, and eventually merging with the red light at your base chakra. As the white light merges with your chakras, it will expand and energize them. Take your time here, as this exercise is highly powerful and shouldn't be rushed.

Visualize a small orange light in your sacral center and see it begin to slowly expand and grow in size. As before, bring up the white light, but this time it should move *through* your red base chakra and into your orange sacral chakra.

Continue in this manner, moving one by one through all your chakras. Bring up the white light from the earth, through your base chakra, and then through all your chakras in sequential order. Focusing on your breath will help raise the energy to each center.

Once you've opened all the chakras, take a moment to run the energy right up to the top of your crown chakra. Take note of this amazing feeling, in which all your centers are open and pulsating simultaneously.

Now place your awareness on your crown chakra and imagine that there's a big funnel reaching out to the universe. This time, see a *new* bright white light begin to form above and slowly pour down through this center, as it meets and merges with the white light from below. Allow these two white lights to blend and become one, and let the intensity of light fill your psychic centers with even more energy.

Take a moment to notice how your aura expands naturally so that you feel as though all the natural boundaries just disappear. This is what's known as *being open*.

You can remain this way until you're ready to start the closing-down process.

Closing down the chakras: Once again, you're going to use the power of thought to close down each chakra, one by one.

When you're ready, bring your attention to the white light from above, which continues to pour through your open crown chakra. Now bring your awareness to your third-eye chakra. Make the expanded indigo light (the corresponding color) smaller and smaller. You should feel the power begin to diminish as you move down to your throat chakra and its pale-blue light. Focus on this light getting smaller, and then move on down to the heart, solar-plexus, and sacral centers. All the different colored lights should be smaller now, resulting in what's known as *being closed*. But remember, you need to keep the crown and base chakras open for a continued flow of energy throughout your system.

Opening and closing your psychic centers is an essential exercise if you wish to continue to safely develop your psychic and intuitive abilities; trust me when I say that there's no way around it. This is the number-one exercise that I regularly practice (before and after all psychic and mediumship work) and teach in my workshops.

———

Your psychic strengths, aura, and chakras are key when practicing or using your psychic or mediumship abilities. I think I've stressed it enough how strongly I feel about education and understanding how the mechanics of your spiritual abilities work. If you honor this, you'll not only become a strong, grounded, and healthier psychic or medium, you'll also be a wise one!

Chapter 11

CONTINUING YOUR JOURNEY

Discovering who we are and what we want are constant endeavors for most of us. We all have our own individual mission for our time here in this physical realm, and with each mission, there are many paths that can lead or guide us to it. There is help to put us on the right path; we have to understand, recognize, and trust that we're never truly alone during our time here. Your intuition, certain people, spirits, guides, and even synchronicity want to help you, and together they can be your partners in discovering what you want and what you need when it comes to the unfoldment of your spiritual abilities.

Can you create or manifest this assistance into your life? *Yes*, you can.

I know for a fact that everyone and everything is surrounded by an aura of magnetic energy. All thoughts, emotions, and feelings are contained in the aura and are sent out to the universe. To put it simply — *what we think is what we attract*. For example, if you're afraid, you'll attract fear; if you're kind, you'll attract kindness; when you're grateful, you'll attract prosperity; and when you're seeking knowledge for the highest good, then the teachers and paths will begin to show up in your life. You'll have free will in choosing to take that all-important first step.

When I spent my time in England, developing and honing my mediumship skills, I was led to the right places and connected with the right people just when I needed them to help me on this wonderful journey. All my thoughts were focused on understanding the workings of psychic ability, mediumship, and being of service to Spirit in the best way that I could. The Spirit World and synchronicity worked in partnership to help guide me so I knew where I needed to be and what I had to do next. But I knew that it was up to me to begin by taking those first steps of trusting in this much-needed guidance. The only way to meet it halfway was not only by studying, but also by actually *doing* the work. I liken this to the analogy of studying to become an actor. You can take all the acting classes you want, but eventually you have to get onstage and perform and perfect your craft! Only then are you able to work out where you need more attention.

CONTINUING YOUR STUDY

When people study with me, whether it's a weekend workshop, a five-day retreat, or sitting in a development circle, they usually ask, "What do we do now?" I reply by saying, "Continue to study and just do the work."

Doing the work means sitting in a mediumship development circle and practicing your mediumship. If you choose to continue on the journey of being a medium, you'll have to really learn and practice to discriminate between the promptings of your own mind and that which is coming from the spiritual realms. It's not always an easy task, but with time it does get easier.

When you have a solid foundation of the mechanics of your ability, you can begin to do readings for others. It's a good idea to start off by demonstrating your mediumship at a beginners' evening at a Spiritualist church, a new-age bookstore, or a spiritual center that offers psychic and mediumship development. There are many churches and facilities that have fledgling nights where you can practice your skills with an audience and begin to feel what it's like to blend your energy with Spirit. I've included listings in this book to help you find resources in your vicinity.

Practice doing as many readings as you can, even if they are complimentary; when you get proficient, trust me, people will begin to notice and they'll reach out to you for help. I now appreciate how each and every reading I gave as practice was a wonderful learning tool for me.

It's well worth trying to study with a number of teachers, if you can. When students come back time after time to study with me, I always advise them that no one person can teach them everything, and I encourage them to work with other experienced teachers and mediums. Working with different tutors can expose you to a broad range of teaching styles, techniques, and lessons. It may be that one instructor may not feel right for you, or they've taught you all that they could and you need a fresh perspective.

The commitment to the unfoldment of your spiritual abilities is up to you, and after practicing and doing your mediumship or psychic development work, you'll begin to appreciate just how *your* spiritual faculties work, which in turn builds your confidence. Never lose the excitement of exploring and learning new things! A Chinese proverb I heard once sums it up beautifully: "Learning is a treasure that will follow its owner everywhere." Never a truer word said. In the following section, I want to give you some helpful advice on the continuation of your journey.

SPIRIT GUIDES & THEIR ROLES

Just as we have friends and teachers in this life who help, support, and inspire us, we also have special assistance from those who work with us from the spiritual realm. They come in the form of our guides and spirit helpers. They're here to guide and assist you, and to help you with your spiritual development. They're *not* in your life to help with mundane things that you need to figure out for yourself. Guides can help to inspire and to put you in the right place at the right time. You'll find them in that still space, the small voice you hear in your head, or in that gut feeling that suddenly comes to you.

Guides also bring people into your life who might help you. If you're studying psychic or mediumship development, then it's likely that you're already aware of your guides.

We all have one main guide who stays with us for our whole life. I have one guide, a Tibetan monk, who's been my main teaching guide since birth. Over the years, I've had many mediums tell me about him, and even had a spirit artist draw his likeness. People often want to know the name of their guides, and if you feel that it's important, then I encourage you to work on receiving their name — or give them one yourself! They're not concerned if you don't know their name, just that you acknowledge them and begin to work in partnership with them.

Besides our main guide, we have others who have their own individual jobs and roles to play. Unlike our main guide, these guides come and go, depending on the need at any one time. I know I have an "inspiration guide" who helps me with my writing, and frequently offers me words of wisdom when I least expect it. I believe that when psychic artists work, they're working with their spirit guides, who most likely were also artists themselves or worked in some other creative way while they were on earth.

Equally, there are healers who have a medical guide or a spirit doctor who works with them while they're seeing patients here. Many medically trained doctors probably have a medical guide/ spirit doctor assisting and working with them and aren't even aware of it.

Imagine the scenario when a doctor is operating on a patient. Even though they have all the patient's medical records, lab tests, and diagnosis, something doesn't *feel* right. The doctor goes on to investigate another area of the body, only to find out that the lab tests missed something — even the main issue of why the patient is really ill. Now, was it the doctor's education, training, and intuition, or was it a guide working side by side with the doctor who put that thought into the doctor's mind? Maybe it was both. It's scenarios like this that make me wonder — and even more curious.

My "Raising the Power" meditation (in Chapter 10) can be used to help you connect with your guides. But please don't have preconceptions of how they will appear to you. You may receive an image, a color, or a feeling, or you may experience beautiful warmth across your shoulders. They're your guides and will come through to you in their own unique and personal way.

It's okay to ask your guides in the meditation, "How will I know you?" Once you've formed a connection with your guide, they'll usually come through the same way every time so you'll know when they're with you. When you feel like you're talking to your guides and you want some evidence that it's really them, just ask them to show you a sign. When I'm about to do a demonstration of mediumship, I often see the number 419. It's not that I'm superstitious in that I have to see or find that number, but I have noticed that this special sign shows up every time I work. It's my guides' personal way of saying, "John, we're here!"

All information and inspiration from your guides should *always* be positive and uplifting. If you experience a so-called guide telling you to do something you wouldn't normally do, it's more than likely your imagination, a fear, or a psychological issue that may need to be addressed. There are many books and websites on guides, so I encourage you to study what feels right to you as you develop your relationship with your guides. You may not always *feel* them, but they're there working behind the scenes and waiting for you to acknowledge and ask for their divine assistance. Get to know them and let them guide and help you.

Seeing the Face of My Guides

Let me share with you the first time I had the wonderful opportunity to see my guide's face. Earlier I briefly wrote about

Coral Polge, the psychic artist from the U.K. whom I was blessed to spend some time with before she passed. She certainly showed me how to appreciate the relationship I have with my guides and their role in my spiritual life.

I remember sitting there in that small room at the Spiritualist Association of Great Britain (SAGB) in London, thinking what better way to be introduced to one of my guides than to have Coral actually draw him!

I sat there quietly; she knew nothing about me, and I didn't know who she was about to draw. She first drew an elderly woman who was related to my mom's side of the family. She even knew that this lovely older woman was from Italy, where my mom's relatives were from. She handed me the drawing, and then something different happened. She picked up color pastels and started a new drawing, saying that a guide wanted to step forward. I was elated!

As my guide linked with Coral, I was suddenly acutely aware that the atmosphere seemed to change in the room. A sense of total peace washed over my entire body, and I could literally feel the emotion of pure love wrap its arms around me. The noise of the city from the outside seemed to fade away and the room became quiet. I could tell that my guide was sending his thoughts to Coral as well. She continued to draw and gently talk to me at the same time, saying, "John, you know he's been with you throughout your life, and he's been assisting you with your mediumship and acting as a teacher for you in this lifetime."

As she was drawing, all I could think about was how I had always been drawn to Tibet and the beautiful Himalayas. The country and its people seem to resonate with me. As a child, I'd often dream of praying men with shaved heads and colorful orange robes, who I now recognize as Tibetan monks. (Little did I know that one of them was about to be revealed as *my* guide!) I vowed that someday I'd visit that extraordinary country. I don't know why, but even today, I really feel as though I've lived there at one time, and I most likely was a Tibetan monk myself.

Time seemed to stand still as Coral drew. When she was almost finished, she gave me more information about where Spirit and my mediumship would take me, and the work that I still had to accomplish.

When she turned her drawing pad around and handed me the portrait of my Tibetan guide, his face seemed so familiar. I noticed his eyes the most. They were the gentlest eyes I'd ever seen. They seemed to reach out to me and touch my very soul. I felt a single tear trickle down my face. My emotions were flooding to the surface as I realized that this beautiful man had been with me my whole life. Somehow, he'd always been there, never intruding or demanding, but gently guiding me.

Coral could see how overwhelmed I was and quietly asked if I was okay. "Yes, Coral, I'm just filled with so many emotions right now; first just having the honor of sitting with you, and now seeing the face of my guide for the first time," I told her. "I know that we all have guides, but somehow having this experience was what I needed at this moment in my life."

I went on to tell her how I was living in the U.K., far away from home and family. I even told her how I'd spent some time recently wondering whether I was doing the right thing. Part of me questioned where this work was taking me. Seeing my guide's face for the first time put everything into perspective and somehow made it all the more authentic. I felt a sense of ease as all my fears melted away. Once again, here was the lesson that I had to learn, namely: Let go and trust. I knew I was on the right path.

I was about to get up, but Coral said she had one more drawing of another guide who really wanted to introduce himself. I didn't need any persuasion and remained firmly seated. She went straight to it, pastels to paper, telling me that this time he was an African shaman and that he'd also been with me for a long time.

"He's telling me, John, that it's his job to protect you and to give you the strength to get through difficult times in your life." Ten minutes later, she showed me the portrait of how he'd chosen to come through with the face markings of an African shaman. He was a big man in stature, but like my Tibetan monk, he had this amazingly friendly face. Now I know why I have so many African masks and art pieces hanging on my walls back home. I gain an inner strength when I look at them. In fact, when we find ourselves drawn to art and foods from other countries, or attracted to the architecture or culture of a specific place, I believe that it may be because of a past-life memory or just that our guides are influencing us.

As I stared at the portrait of my African guide, I realized that he'd been influencing me for some time. It was more a case that I'd not stopped to listen and acknowledge where the influence was coming from.

My time with Coral was just about at an end. I got up to say good-bye, clutching my three portraits. I thanked her profusely and began to walk toward the door, knowing another person was waiting for their sitting. She looked at me and she said very sweetly, "Keep up the good work, young man." I turned back and said, "I will now . . . knowing that I have plenty of help. Good-bye and God bless you."

I've since framed the three drawings that Coral did of my guides, which take pride of place in my meditation room, which also doubles as my studio for my weekly radio show. I think she'd be happy to know they're watching over me when I'm on air! They instill a sense of calmness within me every time I glance at them and I treasure them dearly for so many reasons.

Coral is missed by the thousands here who witnessed her demonstrations of psychic art, and particularly by those like me who she touched personally. I hope that right now, Coral is working with someone here, maybe even an artist, inspiring them, assisting and guiding them on their path. It's further proof that we're all eternal, that we existed before we were born, and will go on long after we leave this physical body.

SITTING IN CIRCLE

In the beginning stages of your psychic development, you'll be developing a more acute state of awareness than you're used to. A lifelong partnership will be formed with the Spirit People as you learn to link and blend more readily with them in this heightened state of awareness. Let me tell you how I prepared myself for this state of heightened awareness.

The best education, training, and practice I experienced while I was studying in England was sitting in a mediumship circle (often known as a development circle). I encourage this for all my students, as well as you, the reader, if you're looking to develop and expand your mediumship potential.

A development circle is when you sit in meditation with a group of other mediums and learn how to connect, reach out, and build a relationship with the Spirit World. It's advantageous to have an experienced medium running the circle who can assist with communication and cooperation with spirit guides and operators. They can also assist you in figuring out (usually in the beginning stages) what's coming from Spirit as opposed to what's coming from your own mind. I knew that sitting with like-minded people would help me in the expansion of my own abilities. I remember the very first time I did it, and how the thought of everyone sharing in each other's psychic energy was a thrilling concept — one I was eagerly looking forward to experiencing.

When sitting in a circle, many people (including myself) experience various forms of psychic manifestations, from a cold breeze, to a slight draft around the feet and legs, to sparkles of light, voices, or even a cobweb-like sensation caressing the skin. The reason for this is that Spirit People use the group's combined psychic energy to draw close and strengthen their connection with the sitters. The first time I experienced this, I wasn't frightened at all, because I was sitting with an experienced group.

Development circles must be harmonious in *all* areas, and you must find the one that works for you. These include open circles (open to everyone), which often take place in a church or a psychic-awareness class. There are also home circles, which are by invitation only. I get lots of e-mails from people who are disappointed that there aren't any Spiritualist churches, psychic centers, or even metaphysical bookstores in their area. I encourage you to do more extensive research. You may be surprised by just how many places there are.

With today's technology, there are online groups that study together and help each other with their abilities. Someone asked me once, "Could an eager student develop on their own?" Yes, of course this is possible, but working with a group of like-minded souls and blending with each other's energy is a better way to build your power as a medium. Plus, it's more beneficial to work with others when developing your mediumship, so that when you do get information from the Spirit World for a circle member, you can practice the whole process of authentication and validation, which is much harder to do in an online forum. Practicing in a live physical environment gives you confidence, and direct feedback confirms whether the information is coming from the Spirit World or from your own mind, or your imagination.

If you absolutely cannot find a development circle, maybe it's time that you started your own. A great book (also published by Hay House) to help you put together your own circle is *Intuitive Studies: A Complete Course in Mediumship*, written by Gordon Smith, a wonderful Scottish medium who was one of my teachers and mentors while I was in England.

I was blessed during my time in England as I was invited to join a home circle for more than two years, where I had thorough, in-depth training with seven fellow circle members. It was an amazing opportunity to share, develop, experiment, and grow in a safe place where we could all review and analyze our experiences. This particular circle was the best spiritual classroom that I've ever attended.

We would meet every Tuesday evening, promptly at 6 P.M., and I remember that if you were tardy, the doors were locked! I considered the development circle as an appointment with Spirit, my loved ones, guides, and spirit helpers. After all, if they could be there on time, then so could I. I'd take a bus from where I was living and always made sure I caught the earlier one, just to be certain!

I remember those first few weeks, learning the ropes, what to do and what not to do, how to behave, and so much more. I was instructed to eat a light meal a couple of hours before we met, because when you are meditating and sitting in the spiritual power of the group, enjoying the blissful peace, nothing is worse than having an empty stomach rumble and disrupt the atmosphere.

In the beginning, I was taught how to expand my aura so that it blended with the aura of the whole circle. The experienced circle leader showed me how to control and direct my thoughts and emotions in a positive manner. She had a beautiful way of teaching that made it feel natural; she would often repeat an exercise several times until she was confident that I was succeeding. The circle only lasted one hour, during which time we were given lessons and set goals for our mediumship techniques. There would be a group meditation to raise our consciousness to invite Spirit People to draw close as we welcomed them into the circle. The second half of the meeting was dedicated to delivering any messages we'd received. Sometimes it would be a message for a circle member, or it would be words of inspiration we'd received from our guides. Every time we met it was always different.

I owe a lot to this development circle as it was the foundation of much of my teachings, where I learned to *feel* what it was like when spirits drew close. I was trained how to reach out and blend with them, and time after time I practiced delivering information and messages that I'd received, so it could be validated. I learned to recognize when my guides were present and to listen and take on board their inspiration and guidance. I truly believe that if you're meant to do this work, you'll be guided to where and what to do next.

If you're looking to join a circle, then please remember that not every circle may *feel* right to you. If you feel it doesn't resonate with you, then I encourage you to find one that feels more in sync with what you're looking for. An experienced medium or teacher should always lead the circle, and the room should be clean and comfortable, with appropriate lighting and music to set the energy for meditation. The other members should also have a positive energy about them and a positive intent, as well as a willingness to support and help each other. Find a good teacher, one who will instruct you in mediumship, one who will teach you safe practices while continually instilling good ethics. Some teachers feel that just sitting in meditation is enough, but I firmly believe that there's a reason why it's called a development circle. I've heard stories about the egos of some circle members disrupting the energy of the group. It's up to the circle leader to keep the group integrated, balanced, and spiritually positive by bringing uniformity and harmony within the circle. Have no worries, you'll find the perfect place for you at the right time.

If you're nervous about joining a circle, any good leader will give you some useful advice to help you connect with the circle seamlessly. They'll more than likely suggest that you try to arrive a little early, so you have time to wind down from your day. That way, you'll join the circle being grounded and less stressed. It's always good to turn up with intent of the highest good. A few more useful tips: Wear comfortable, clean clothing; try not to use perfumes or colognes, since others may be sensitive to them; leave your day and expectations at the door, and walk in with an open, receptive mind and spirit.

Developing with others can be both nurturing and uplifting. You not only have the opportunity to work as a group to build a bridge with Spirit as you become more receptive to spirit contact, but you also get to be part of a mutually supportive spiritual tribe, learning and sharing from each other's experiences. Some of your circle members may just turn out to be your spiritual family and lifelong friends.

Something important to remember: It's possible as you develop your mediumship for your ability to seemingly slow down or even come to a complete halt. This can also be true for working mediums; it's happened to me as well as other mediums I know, but I never panic. I just look at it as if I've reached a certain level, and that something is about to change in my mediumship. It's as though I feel it's an opportunity to acknowledge what I have learned, how far I've come, and to evaluate if there are any lessons that need to be revisited. As you develop, you'll have both the highs and lows, which is to be expected, since mediumship works on an energetic level. Energy constantly changes, moves, and expands, as will your mediumship. Every time you work, it's an opportunity to learn and grow.

If you've been sitting in a development circle or class for a while and you feel there's not enough happening or your abilities are not significantly growing, then it could be due to a number of reasons. It's possible that you're trying to push too hard, or you might not have a strong mediumship potential. It could be the circle is not the right fit, as I've mentioned earlier. It could be that you're too busy in other areas of your life, and that you don't have the capacity at this point.

First and foremost, don't worry! You were born with your own unique and special talents. I know that some of you might be saying, "I thought this was what I was supposed to be doing and I don't know what other talents I have." Go back to your childhood and ask yourself what you loved then or what your passion is now. God gave each and every one of us individual talents to develop and share with others. It's your special gift . . . your signature on the world.

Mediumship is just one of these gifts, but there are so many others, such as writing, music, art, inspirational speaking, and healing. If you have a burning desire in your heart to help others and to be of service, then the Spirit World will identify your skill and guide you to where it can be developed and applied. Just because you're not doing mediumship doesn't mean you're not connected to the Spirit World. It's what you do with what you have that truly matters. Seek your own experiences and you'll attain your own awareness. In turn, you'll be able to make up your own mind about how you want to follow your spiritual path.

THE ENERGY & STRUCTURE OF THE MESSAGE

Almost every medium I know works in their own style and in their own way, as there's no "one size fits all" in the work we do!

When I started out demonstrating my mediumship, my style was somewhat different to what it is today. I was unfamiliar with how Spirit wanted to work with me, and I constantly feared that the link would break before I'd even started. As a result, my style was often fast and furious, as I paced back and forth on the stage. The energy that surged through my body was so strong that my natural response was to keep moving as if I needed to burn off that quickening energy. Anyone would think that I was running a 100-meter sprint race or something. In those early days, as I was figuring out how best to work, it was not only exhausting for me, but I'm sure the audiences felt like they were watching a tennis match. Over time and with the help of teachers and my guides, I finally learned that you don't need to burn the energy but rather use it effectively and sparingly.

I worked in this way for a number of years, constantly learning, refining, and gaining a deeper awareness of how Spirit wanted to work with me. It wasn't necessarily wrong, as we all have our own styles. I was often totally drained by the end of a demonstration after the high from being connected to Spirit had worn off. I consider myself a lifetime student of this work and even though I now have many years of experience, both demonstrating and teaching, even the student can sometimes forget what we were taught.

During my training, I was taught to manage and conserve my energy so that I would have as much power and energy giving the last message as I had giving the first. There were times when I didn't remember these wise words of advice. But as always, the Spirit People would somehow know when I needed to have a *refresher course!* They'd find a suitable opportunity to teach me once again. One of those suitable opportunities came just a few of years ago, when they clearly decided I needed a lesson.

I'd broken a bone in my foot and had to wear a cast for a couple of months. Initially, it was a bit of a talking point, but then I just had to get on and deal with it. I still needed to work and couldn't cancel my public events. I was due to give a lecture and demonstration at an event on the South Shore of Massachusetts. It was my first event where I would be wearing the cast, so I knew that I wouldn't be able to do my usual frenetic pacing back and forth. Somehow, I just knew that the Spirit People would work around it. I hobbled out onstage and explained to the audience why I was wearing the cast (to some amusement) and that I'd be doing the demonstration from my chair.

At the start of the demonstration, I gave my brief lecture explaining how it all works so the audience would have a better understanding. I told them what they could expect, how their loved ones are really okay, and how they would be able to recognize the signs sent from spirits to confirm they're often around us at special times. The purpose of the introductory lecture is to educate everyone about the process of mediumship and the afterlife so that even those who won't leave with a message will have something to go home with. I like everyone to leave my demonstrations with a sense of hope and inspiration. Sometimes my words can be just enough to help them move on. When people hear a message that someone else is receiving, it can act as a sort of confirmation about the continuity of life, and bring comfort in the knowledge that their own loved ones who have passed also still exist.

As I was sitting there with my cast, I could feel the Spirit People drawing close. Anyone who knows me has heard me say, "It's crowded up here!" even though it's just me they see! But it can feel like there's a full cast onstage, all patiently waiting their turn to speak. The messages were coming in one after the other and were very strong. It quickly dawned on me that it wasn't necessary to pace about the stage to keep the energy flowing, that sitting there was just as powerful and, if anything, the link with the Spirit People was even stronger. I realized that the energy I used up pacing around the stage was now being used to bring through spirits with good evidence and validation. They were providing me with lots of details about their personalities, habits, and personal stories to confirm their identities.

Today, when I work I no longer pace back and forth, but it's more like a slow stroll to see the audience. I've learned to manage my energy, to remain still and use that precious energy to make my mediumship clearer, stronger, and more meaningful. It took a broken bone in my foot to learn this lesson and become a better medium. I'm better and wiser because of the experience. There's always a lesson to learn, whether you feel an experience is negative or positive. It's the fact that you've learned something that truly matters. What I learned that evening about how to conserve my energy I've now added to the teaching techniques in my workshops.

THE C.E.R.T. FORMULA FOR DELIVERING MESSAGES

As a teacher, I spend a lot of time explaining to developing students the importance of delivering messages that have a flow and structure to them. You always know when a medium hasn't been trained properly, as they tend to flit back and forth with information, often mixing up messages from different Spirit People. It's hard to follow them, and it's difficult for the recipients to authenticate the link. Messages can get muddled and lose their meaning.

There's a lot of energy going through the medium once the link is secured, and when you combine the fact that the person receiving the message may be nervous, unable to respond as fast as the medium is working, it can easily unravel. This is why I feel that working to a tried-and-tested formula when delivering messages not only helps the person receiving the message, but also helps the medium's energy to remain constant and continuous.

One of the best message-delivery methods I know of — the C.E.R.T. Formula — is one I learned while I was a student. This unique way of giving a message using a set structure is from a brilliant Welsh medium named Stephen O'Brien. I had the amazing opportunity and honor to see him live onstage, working together with Coral Polge in the U.K. He would bring through the evidence of a Spirit Person, and she would start to draw the person he was linking with. Such a great thing to watch as they worked in tandem to bring forth the Spirit People.

Now back to the C.E.R.T. formula. Although many British mediums work this way, it was Stephen who gave it an explanation and a name. I now use this formula when teaching, and if you're studying and developing your mediumship ability, I urge you to try work with this formula. As a result, the Spirit People know how you want to work and will do their best to work with you.

This helpful formula provides sequential order to the spirit contact, by confirming who they are and why they've come forward to the loved one or friend who's receiving the message. This formula is intended to be done in order, so there's a logical and natural flow to the message. Here's what each letter of the C.E.R.T. Formula stands for.

- **C = Communicator:** This is all about confirming the identity of the spirit. The communicating spirit will send information to confirm whether they're male or female, adult or child, the age when they passed, and how they died. Often other information, such as physical descriptions and the relationship to the person receiving the message, comes through.

- **E = Evidence:** Once the spirit is identified, more evidence comes through to validate the message. The information can include names, hobbies, special memories, character traits, or personal mannerisms. Equally, geographical information, important dates, pets, and often proof that they're aware of what's happening in the recipient's life will come through. Building the evidence is vital because it will enable the Spirit World to build a bridge upon which love will pass. This is all part of the process of validation of the loved one who's coming through.

- **R = Return:** Why has the spirit chosen to return with a message at this time? This is when the medium can give a heartfelt message. It could be a message of reassurance that they're still around their loved ones. It could be a message of forgiveness, love, and support, as well as guidance. Heartfelt messages can touch the lives of those here who may be suffering from bereavement. Messages not only affect the recipient, but if a message is given in a public forum, the whole audience benefits in the knowledge that their loved ones also go on and are safe.

- **T = Tie It Up:** The final part of the formula is all about tying up any loose ends and putting the whole message together. Sometimes the medium might revisit all or just a portion of the information that has been given. This is also when the medium has the opportunity to quickly place a piece of evidence that the recipient didn't understand earlier. The sitter shouldn't ever go home with more nos than yeses. Final words of love are usually passed on at this point. Then move on to the next reading.

I want to share the following true story to offer a deeper understanding of how the formula works when giving a message. I've given many messages throughout my career, and since they are coming *through* me and not *from* me, many will fade from my memory because they are meant to be messages that are passed on to others and not meant for me to hold on to. But occasionally there are some Spirit People and messages that are so extraordinary, that they stick in my memory for a long time.

If I were to use this reading as an example of the C.E.R.T. Formula, then it could be broken into the various parts this way:

The Communicator

It was a beautiful fall day in Arizona, and I was invited to be a guest medium at an After-Life Convention. The conference featured many speakers, such as mediums, grief experts, shamans, scientists, scholars, therapists, medical doctors, nurses, and hospice workers. The goal of the conference is to provide wisdom and support for those dealing with the end of life, and also to increase awareness of life beyond the physical body, through a mystical approach to death and bereavement.

This particular afternoon it was my job to demonstrate spirit communication through mediumship, as some of the hundreds of people in the audience had never seen a medium work in person before. I began with my usual brief introduction of how I work and what they can expect during the demonstration. Immediately, I felt the spirit of a quite happy man coming through. I felt I was talking to a gentleman who was larger than life; I couldn't stop smiling when I linked with him. This is a man who loved life and his wife, and everyone loved him. When he was in your presence, he simply made you feel happy.

It was time to give off what I was receiving: "Hi, everyone! I've got a great guy coming through with quite the personality! He's making me feel so joyful, and he was known for being perpetually happy. I feel like this man passed from a sudden heart attack in his 70s. He wants to reach out to his wife. I keep also hearing a name . . . It sounds like Tina, Tiny, Tony, Tino. I know there's a *t* and an *n* in a short name."

The crowd was big, but I did see a woman raise her hand. I said to her, "Hello, darling, do you understand what he's saying?"

She began to laugh, and the whole group turned to listen as she spoke. "My name is Lori, and my husband passed last year from a heart attack at 77. He was a very happy guy, and everybody loved him! His name was Tino."

"Great!" I replied.

As I continued talking to his wife, Lori, I felt he was quite a lover of big cars, as he was showing himself in my mind's eye being happy and relaxed, driving a large Cadillac. I continued with the reading: "He's now showing himself driving quite the big Cadillac! Would you understand that?"

Lori immediately replied, "Oh, he loved his big cars!" Lori and the audience were amused because I could feel myself taking on his mannerisms. I actually started to act as if I were him, driving the car and smiling just like he would do. He was linking and blending with me so closely that I couldn't help but be overshadowed by his spirit and personality.

"He is also talking about something that has to do with charities. Do you understand that?" I asked.

"No, John, I don't understand that one."

"Okay," I told her. "I'll leave it for now."

"One last thing he is making me so very aware of. He must have been married a few times, because he's telling me: When he married you — he finally got it right! Do you understand that?"

Lori smiled and chuckled. "Yes, John. I was his fourth wife, and he *did* get it right!" As I ended, all I could keep expressing was the love he had for Lori. "Wow! He so loves you and still does from the Other-Side! Thank you, Lori, for working with me."

The Evidence

In my mind, he was showing me both of his feet, although I was a little confused, as it appeared he had feet without any toes! This could mean one of two things as Spirit taps into my life experiences, which I will explain. He was quite clever as he was using my memories to provide more evidence to his wife that it really was him, Tino.

"Darlin', I can feel the love and joy he brought you as well as so many others. What a pleasure it is linking with him! Would you understand that Tino loved the water?"

"Yes! Yes!" his wife replied. Her continually nodding face was validation enough.

"Now he's showing me something that I don't understand. He's making me feel like he not only had missing toes on both his feet, but he actually had half of both feet cut off. Do you understand that?"

"Yes, totally. He had to have half of his feet removed because he developed severe diabetes," she confirmed.

The audience had no idea what was going in my mind as I am blending with Tino. In my mind, I got the image of scuba diving.

I immediately knew (being a certified diver myself) that he also loved the water. Once again, he was using my own personal memories and visual database for evidence.

I always deliver a message as it comes through without over-analyzing the information, so I continued. "He's now showing me how much he enjoyed hanging out in his swimming pool, and I'm asking him how he could do that with only half of his feet and his diabetic wounds. But he's showing me a piece of equipment that was specially made for him so he could continue with his love of swimming. Does that make sense?"

I could tell that everyone in the audience was enjoying and loving Tino as much as I was!

"Yes, John. He had a special rubber boot he wore that provided a tight seal around his lower legs and kept his feet completely waterproof."

The Return

"Wow! I love this guy!" I continued. "He wants you to know that even though he's passed, you still need to continue living your life and to make sure you have a good time doing it! He wants me to thank you for all you have done for him and he's telling me that he was the luckiest guy on earth when he met you. He knows how much you miss him but he wants you to go on! He says he'll be waiting for you when it's your time many years from now. He hasn't gone anywhere — he's still very close to you and will love you always."

Tie It Up

I said, "So, as I begin to close the link with him, you understand how he loved you so very much; his love of life, always ready to throw a party with all the drinks and snacks around the pool; his love of cars; and that even with only half of his feet, he still played golf and lived a full life, continuing to do everything he loved. Yes?"

"Oh, yes!" she replied.

"Remember when I was saying he mentioned charities and you didn't understand that?"

"Yes," she said.

"I think he's referencing a foundation that he was associated with?"

"That I understand. He helped start a foundation that is dedicated to helping the ecosystem of Lake Ilopango in El Salvador, " she said, smiling.

I told her what a pleasure it had been linking with Tino to give her such a special message. I ended by telling her, "He's as much alive as he was here. As a matter of fact, I think he's even more alive over there! Once again, he's sending his love to you. Thank you again for working with me. God bless."

When delivering messages with a formula that has structure to it, everyone benefits. Your energy is being conserved, and the recipient can usually remember the message in its entirety instead of in fragmented bits and pieces. When it's in front of an audience, they too benefit because they can follow along and understand how it all works. Try this formula for yourself. It's not the only way, but if you find it beneficial, let the Spirit People know that this is what you're striving for in working with your mediumship.

THE ETHICS & MORALS OF MEDIUMSHIP

To be of service to those who dwell in the Spirit World, as well as to those who reside here in the physical realm is a sacred calling and should be treated as such. Mediumship, when practiced professionally, should be regarded as a most honorable dedicated life of service.

People seek out mediums for many reasons. Some are suffering a loss and are in a state of bereavement, while others might be looking for spiritual guidance. No matter what they're seeking, it's our job as true professionals to appreciate the sensitivity that's needed from us. People often come to us hoping that we'll be able to help them anyway we can. The burden and responsibility for us to deliver the desired outcome is immense. If we're having an off day and the link can't be created, or someone else comes through instead of the person they wanted, the disappointment is clear to see. Yet, when the link is strong and the message is on point, the sense of comfort, closure, and healing is a joy to witness. We must try to help if we're able and treat those who seek our counsel with the utmost compassion and care. Every medium should strive to be a medium of the highest caliber of morals and ethics.

I consider being able to communicate with the spiritual realm both an honor and a gift. As I've said before, the ability doesn't come from us. We may be the vessel, having learned the mechanics by which spirit communication flows, but we must remember that this ability comes from God, the Source, a higher power, or whatever name you prefer to use. As a result, we must try to put ourselves aside and not let our egos exploit what's honorable and sacred. Whenever I'm doing this work, I encourage people to remain humble, thankful, and respectful for their spiritual abilities, and to always have gratitude in their hearts. Remember, we're trying to bridge this world with those living in the Spirit World by raising the consciousness of ourselves, and hopefully of those we're being of service to.

In this closing section of the book, I hope that all my advice as well as the information I've imparted will help you (if you're either a practicing medium or developing) when working with others. We must remember that when someone reaches out for help, whether it's their first time or they've consulted mediums in the past, that they're vulnerable and many emotions could arise during their session. Being compassionate will help the person find closure and healing; often that one reading can open up a whole new world to them. It can even help them to connect to their own spiritual power and purpose as they continue through their own life.

What Are the Ethics and Morals for Mediums?

I try to practice what I preach, and I believe passionately in having strong ethics. I always spend a significant part of my teaching workshops instilling the following ethics into my students.

- Honesty is an absolute must.

- Work with the highest integrity and best intentions for all involved.

- Call on the universal white light to surround you, and request that only the highest good can come through.

- Every private reading should be treated as confidential.

- Mediums should not give predictions. Learn to discern what is "psychic" information and what is "spirit" communication. If you're working on a psychic level, advise the client that the information is *not* from Spirit, but rather intuitive information, and that the future is not set in stone; instill the importance of free will.

- Don't make the person who seeks you out believe that you are the only one who can help them. Make people aware that you are just like them; you are not all-knowing. It's okay to assist when you can, but mediums should not let people become dependent on them. Do the best job you can with care and compassion, and then it's up to the person to try to move on with the knowledge that their loved one who has passed is still alive in the Spirit World and part of their lives. Some may need additional bereavement counseling with a properly trained therapist.

- Don't make exaggerated claims. No medium can guarantee that a specific spirit will come through.

- Don't predict a death. I myself have never received this kind of information during a reading, but I was inspired one time and said to someone, "Go visit your grandmother." Three months later the woman's grandmother did pass, and if I hadn't said that, the visit wouldn't have happened in time. I didn't know, nor was I given the knowledge, that she was going to pass, I just felt inspired to say the words.

- Don't embellish a message. Don't try to add more information that's not there to make it come across as more interesting.

- Don't put your "stuff" into the message. Messages don't need to be speckled with the medium's personal opinion and beliefs.

- When giving information, remember: *impression* vs. *expression*. There are ways to say things to people. For example: If you're *impressed* with seeing a scene of someone passing tragically, then be careful how you *express* the information to the sitter. They may still be emotional and going through bereavement. They don't need to relive that experience again. An inherent sensitive nature is a great asset to a medium.

- Don't walk up to a total stranger and deliver an unsolicited reading. They're not expecting it. Always have utmost respect for other people's faith and beliefs, as well as their privacy.

- Don't play doctor! If you have any concern about a person's health, it's not your job (unless you have a medical degree) to give a proper diagnosis. Always advise the person to seek out medical assistance.

- A medium should never conduct spirit communication while under the influence of drugs or alcohol.

- Know when a person needs a therapist as opposed to a medium.

- Take a bereavement class to become even more enlightened and helpful to those you're delivering messages to. You're not a counselor, but it's always good to understand the process of bereavement.

As a medium who practices good ethics and morals, you'll earn respect not only from the public who seek you out, but equally from those in the Spirit World. You will quickly become a revered and respected medium and one of total integrity. I'm a big believer of "What you sow, you reap."

In other words, do good work, remain humble, have gratitude, and give back when you can. When you do this, not only will the blessings from the universe and Heaven come back to you when you share your gifts, talents, and abilities, but it may assist other people in revealing their own.

———

I hope that by reading this book, you've found some comfort and healing with the knowledge that your loved ones are healthy, vibrant, and quite alive, and you are always connected. I also hope I've showed that it's still possible to have your own loving connection with them. If you read this material so you can become more psychically perceptive or to develop your mediumship potential, then please continue to study and grow, so you can move forward with humility and grace. Try to be the best medium you can be and stay grounded, so you can be of service to those in the spiritual realm as well as those who are here. Remember there are many different gifts of the Spirit. To one may be given the word of wisdom, to another knowledge and inspiration, to another the gift of healing. Whatever gifts you have been given, it's what you do with them that truly matters.

One of my goals in writing this book was to broaden your perceptions and help you appreciate the truth. There is no death; what we call "death" is actually the Other-Side of life. I also wanted to show you how magnificently sentient we are, and how we have everything we need within us to develop and enhance our spiritual abilities. Learn to let go of what you believe our limitations are as humans. We are all made up of the same divine energy that permeates everything here in this physical realm as well as the Other-Side.

Over the forthcoming days and weeks ahead, try to remember to look for the beauty in all things. Too many of us take things for granted. Make an effort whenever you look at anything physical to also try to see and feel the beautiful life force, the spirit within and around all things — be it a person, an animal, a flower, a tree, or even nature itself. As you continue to develop your spiritual inner self and cultivate your abilities, you'll build your own special bridge that will enable you to journey beyond the constraints of the physical world. You'll discover spiritual realms and realities that you had previously been unaware of. As your abilities grow, you'll be helping not only yourself but also many others. Peace, harmony, and beauty will enter your life; this, in turn, will create a positive ripple effect that reaches farther than you could ever imagine.

Go forth now. Stay grounded and open up your heart,
mind, and soul so you can perceive and understand
these truths for yourself through your own experiences.
I wish you well and much happiness on your journey.

All my blessings,

John

EPILOGUE

The Gift

Fall 2014. Boston.

The air in New England this special day was crisp, and the glorious fall foliage had my senses perked as I crunched over frosted leaves that made a kaleidoscope of yellows, reds, and oranges. I was on my way to a big event in Boston at the historic Back Bay Center. Dr. Brian Weiss and I were there to speak individually to a crowd of over 1,000 people who wanted to understand past lives, and I was to help them communicate with those who passed over, but I had a little time to deal with my daily to-do list. (As hard as it might be to believe, those who communicate with the Spirit World also have to deal with regular "stuff" like groceries, working out, and buying birthday cards for friends.) I was pushing it because a good friend's big day was right around the corner. Luckily, I ran into a quaint Hallmark store and popped in to buy a birthday card.

I was in the birthday aisle, trying to find the right saying, when I heard it. It spoke *clearly* in my head.

Buy a Snoopy.

What? One more time.

Buy a Snoopy.

I'm not someone who goes around buying small plush toys. Then again, I wasn't really questioning those three words. I never do because I'm here, mind open. It wasn't long before I found my feet wandering and my hands reaching for a small Snoopy stuffed toy. At the time, there were more questions than answers.

Who was the owner?

When would I put it in his or her hands?

Is this going to a child, or am I being instructed from a child in Spirit?

As usual with the Spirit World, I would have to allow the story to unfold.

Back at the convention center, Brian did a wonderful job explaining reincarnation and doing a group regression where people could experience a past-life memory. Then I heard the words, "Ladies and gentlemen, please welcome best-selling author, psychic medium, and spiritual teacher, John Holland." I heard the thunderous applause of 1,100 or so clapping hands and walked out into the bright lights. My eyes gazed at an audience that was more than ready for me to tell them something life changing. What would happen — what *could* happen — was anyone's guess. When you are doing mediumship work, you never know what may transpire or who is going to come through. It's the exciting part of the job, but at the same time, it can be a little scary. Because we all *hope* it's going to work. It usually always does.

Did I have the Snoopy in my hand? Nope. After I purchased it, I gave it to my assistant, who had put it behind the podium onstage at the event because I didn't want anyone to see it. I thought it was cute when she put a big red bow around the famous beagle's neck. I didn't want to just ask the whole audience: "Does anyone have anything to do with Snoopy?" If I did that, I could imagine how many people would raise their hands because they could associate themselves with the Snoopy reference. I'm sure there would have been many associations with beagles, the name Charlie, or other characters' names from the comic strip. Too many references to consider. Perhaps Snoopy would be going home with me. I had to wait and follow the instruction and guidance from the Spirit Person who told me to buy the doll, which I hoped I would get during the mediumship demonstration. I had to wait and see . . . and trust.

There was no time to dwell on it. The Spirit People drew close. They had arrived.

"I'm given messages," I told the crowd of hopeful faces. Many messages were given that afternoon, one after the other. Parents came through to their children, husbands and wives came through, grandparents sent their love as they gave evidence of their survival. There were laughs as well as tears. So far, it'd been a good afternoon, but I was starting to doubt that the special gift hiding behind the podium would be given out that day.

A thought drifted through my mind as I walked across the long stage, and I addressed the right side of the audience, halfway up the many rows of seats: "Who here in this area has an association with someone that worked for the United States post office? Specifically, I'm seeing the trucks that mailmen and mailwomen drive." A quick scan on my part, and a hand shot up. Only one hand. So I wandered even closer to the edge of the stage and made my way over to a woman named Tracy.

"My grandfather worked for the post office fixing their trucks," she said.

I gently said, "You also lost your mom."

"Lung cancer," she confirmed.

"She says your daughter is here with her."

Tracy's eyes filled with tears. She went on to explain that some years ago, she had a baby daughter who was stillborn.

"She knows that she has two brothers who were born after her, but wants you to know she is safe with her grandmother," I said.

Indeed, Tracy was the mother of two sons who were born after the little girl. This might have been the end of this encounter with a message given from beyond. But it was only the beginning.

"Wait a minute," I said. "Now, they're telling me that somebody you know experienced a loss, and the person who crossed over didn't have a chance to say good-bye. Who didn't get a chance to say good-bye to a mother?"

Tracy didn't hesitate, pointing to her husband, Jeff, who was sitting quietly next to her. He was a tall man, with sadness on his face.

"Sudden heart attack took Mom," Jeff said. "She never had the chance to say good-bye."

His mom came through, and I could feel the strongest bond of love between a mother and son. I even saw the number one appear above his head, which could only mean one of two things: only child or favorite.

"Only child?" I asked.

"No," he said.

"So, you're the favorite?"

"Yes," he said, smiling. Jeff went on to tell me that he never got to see his mother before she left this world, which he knew was not her choice. In fact, his mother was the kind of parent who would do anything to make something better for her child. I knew that because I could hear Mom on the Other-Side telling me that she had a message for her son, but someone else would give it. At that moment, I felt another presence step forward, a spirit standing next to her on the Other-Side. I saw the biggest grin on the face of a man who was obviously Jeff's father.

"Your dad is here," I said.

"Dad passed from Alzheimer's in a veterans' home," Jeff said. "He didn't remember . . ."

A spirit voice suddenly popped into my head that reminded me of what was hiding behind the podium: *This where the Snoopy is supposed to go.*

I quickly sent out a thought to the spirit: *Thank you! I hoped that you would show up today!*

I took a deep breath and said, "I don't usually do this, but every once in a rare while, someone on the Other-Side will ask me to bring a special and distinctive gift to one of my mediumship demonstrations. I never know why or for whom it's intended at the time. I just have to trust. While I was at a store the other day, I heard a voice telling me to buy a special gift." I raced back to the podium to grab the Snoopy and put it behind my back. "I have an odd question for you, Jeff, although maybe there are no odd questions," I said.

Jeff's eyes went wide.

"Do you have anything to do with Snoopy?" I asked as I held it high above my head so he as well as the audience could see it.

The answer on his face was plain.

"Oh. My god! My father knew Charles Schulz," he said. "Every year he would fly to California to play in the Snoopy Hockey Tournament. He worked so much and never took a break unless it was for hockey. He was really good at it, too! He played, coached, and refereed the sport, and he was very involved with youth hockey coaching for many high school teams in our home area. He was past president of the NIHOA, the National Ice Hockey Officials Association. Everyone loved my dad!"

What I didn't know until that moment was that the famed creator of the Peanuts comic loved the sport of hockey so much that he installed a regulation hockey rink right below his office. From 1975 up to this day, he would host the Snoopy Tournament, a major amateur senior ice hockey game, on his property in Santa Rosa, California. Teams from around the world come from near and far to play in this tournament, even if it is for just one day.

"Charles had his own team that played in the tournament, and of course it was called *Team Snoopy*. He would always ask Dad and say, 'Come play for my team,'" Jeff said. "Dad would say with a smile, 'I'm honored, but I can't let my teammates down and go off to play for your team, Charles.'"

"Amazing!" I said. "This is your dad's message: *No more suffering from Alzheimer's. He remembers everything . . . His memory is back*. He's quite a clever spirit. What a dad! So much love is coming from him."

I walked off the stage and gently handed Jeff his special Snoopy gift. Tears were rolling down Jeff's face, and the entire audience was weeping over a small plush toy with a big meaning.

I wonder whether people realize that the Other-Side makes all the arrangements and planning for messages like these. I'll always be astounded whenever it happens. I had to hear the Spirit Person say to buy the Snoopy toy at the perfect time, just when I was in the card store, to get me to bring it and hide it, so it could go exactly to whom it was intended out of 1,100 people! This is yet another example of how they do, in fact, see and feel what is going on with us here. Jeff's dad knew his son and wife were coming to this event and took full advantage of the opportunity! I know that all messages can be unique and wonderful, but when I'm told to bring a certain gift, I know these messages are even more special. I can take some of the credit, but really, it's the Spirit World that does most of the work.

As for Jeff, a grown man suddenly held a precious link between the two realms, one that he and his family will treasure and never forget for the rest of their lives — and neither will I.

I want you to remember that there is no such thing as "gone." Love is the bridge.

I want you to know that they are with you. Always.

I want you to watch for the messengers like me. Look for the signs. Feel the love.

It finds a way . . .

GLOSSARY

absent healing: Spiritual energy combined with healing thoughts from a healer sent to a patient many miles away.

after-death communication (ADC): Also known as calling cards, these are signs and symbols sent to us by spirits on the Other-Side. These experiences come in many forms, often quite personal, but always loving, joyful, and positive.

afterlife: The state of existence after our time in physical bodies on earth.

angel: A higher being that exists on the Celestial Plane.

apport: An item brought through from the Spirit World.

astral body: The spiritual body we'll inhabit after death, visible by some clairvoyants. The astral body is part of the Astral Plane.

Astral Plane: The plane we gravitate toward after death. Also known as the *Summerland*.

aura: The subtle energetic field that surrounds everything and everyone. The human aura, which surrounds the body, contains information about who we are.

calling card: *see* after-death communication

Celestial Plane: The highest, least dense plane of existence, where time and space are irrelevant. The dwelling place of ascended masters, teachers, celestial beings, guides, and angels.

chakra: An energy center of the body. There are seven major chakras (as well as many minor ones) that play an important function in our physical and spiritual lives.

chi: *see* prana

clairaudience: The psychic ability to receive information through hearing it subjectively (within the mind) or objectively (from outside).

"clairs": A collective nickname for the powers of clairaudience, clairsentience, and clairvoyance.

clairsentience: The psychic ability to receive information through feeling and simply knowing the information.

clairvoyance: The psychic ability to receive information through seeing signs and symbols.

deathbed vision (DBV): A phenomenon some people experience just before they pass in which they experience a visitation from Spirit.

development circle: Also known as a meditation circle, this is when we sit in meditation with a group of other mediums and learn how to connect, reach out, and build a relationship with the Spirit World.

discarnate: The state of being a spirit not in a physical body; a Spirit Person. (*also see* incarnate)

Earth: The Physical Plane of existence where we live when we're alive.

ectoplasm: Spiritual matter; a white substance that appears to stream out of the body of some mediums during a séance. It can form itself into a materialized spirit or part of a spirit.

electronic voice phenomenon (EVP): Sounds from Spirit, recorded electronically but not audible to the human ear.

empathic: Able to pick up on the emotions of others.

energy center: *see* chakra

etheric body: This spiritual body serves as the link between the physical body and astral body. It draws in *prana* (life-giving energy).

etheric cord: The cord that connects our spirit to our physical body while we sleep, as our spirit is visiting the Spirit World for rejuvenation.

Etheric Plane: The plane next to the Physical Plane, the start of the nonphysical world and the universe.

guide: *see* spirit guide

incarnate: The state of being a spirit in a physical body. (*also see* discarnate)

intuition: The ability to receive information out of the blue in the form of a hunch or gentle nudge.

karmic lesson: Something that you are meant to learn in this lifetime due to agreements you made in the Spirit World or because of something that happened in another lifetime.

life review: A process that the soul goes through after leaving the physical body (whether through death or a near-death experience) in which you experience for yourself every feeling that you caused others in your lifetime.

medium: Someone who connects with and passes on information from the Other-Side. All mediums are psychic, but not all psychics are mediums.

mediumship circle: *see* development circle

mental body: The second-highest of the spiritual bodies.

Mental Plane: One of the higher, least dense planes of existence. In this plane, energy moves beyond the concept of speed, and objects and things do not stay in any one form.

meridian: A network of internal systems of the body.

mind-to-mind communication: *see* thought transference

near-death experience (NDE): An experience that happens when a person is close to death, where the spirit leaves the physical body.

Other-Side: *see* Spirit World

physical body: The body that we inhabit while living on the Physical Plane (earth).

Physical Plane: The physical world in which we live; earth. The densest of the planes of existence.

prana: Life-giving energy, the universal life force that runs through everything, including ourselves. Also referred to as *spiritual energy* or *chi* in Traditional Chinese Medicine.

pre-birth experience (PBE): A memory of conditions from before birth, either on earth or on the Other-Side.

psychic: The ability to access, receive, and transmit information from a person's aura or from items they're holding that belong to the person they're reading. (All mediums are psychic, but not all psychics are mediums.)

psychic database: Memories, images, symbols, and signs that have specific, personalized meanings for you. You can draw on your psychic database to interpret messages from the Other-Side.

shared-death experience (SDE): A phenomenon some people experience in which they share the initial transition of a dying person passing from this physical world to the next.

silver cord: *see* etheric cord

soul: Used interchangeably with *spirit*. The soul is the real you — pure consciousness.

soul-to-soul connection: A form of telepathy or thought trans-ference in which another soul on earth or on the Other-Side con-nects with your mind.

Source: Another name for Universe, God, Spirit, Creator, higher power.

Spirit: With an uppercase *S*, this word refers to God, the Divine Source, the Universe. A spark of Spirit dwells in each of us.

spirit: With a lowercase *s*, this word is meant to be defined as an individual who no longer has a physical body. This is one who dwells in the Spirit World.

spirit guide: Beings from the Spirit World who help us with our spiritual development through inspiring us and guiding us through important life events.

Spirit People: Another name for the spirits who are communicat-ing to us in the Physical Realm.

spiritual body: The highest body, connected to the most evolved planes of existence. Mediums and spirits communicate through this body.

spiritual energy: *see* prana

Spirit World: Our real home, the realm where our passed-over loved ones as well as ascended masters, teachers, celestial beings, guides, and angels dwell. Other names for this realm include *Other-Side, Heaven, Paradise, Eternity,* and *Upstairs.* The Spirit World encompasses all the planes of existence.

Summerland: *see* Astral Plane

telepathy: The ability to send and receive messages and informa-tion through the mind.

Thin Place: A peaceful, tranquil place where we feel closer to God, Spirit, Heaven. Name comes from the Celtic tradition.

thought transference: An exchange of energy that acts as a com-munication link without using the physical senses.

RECOMMENDED
RESOURCES & READING

BOOKS

Beginner's Guide to Mediumship by Larry Dreller (Samuel Weiser, 1997)

The Complete Idiot's Guide to Communicating with Spirits by Rita Berkowitz and Deborah S. Romaine (Alpha, 2003)

Contacting the Spirit World by Linda Williamson (Piatkus, 1996)

Dying to Be Me by Anita Moorjani (Hay House, 2014)

The Fun of Staying in Touch by Roberta Grimes (CreateSpace Independent Publishing, 2014)

Glimpses of Eternity by Raymond Moody, M.D. (Sakkara Productions, 2016)

The Grief Recovery Handbook by John W. James and Russell Friedman (Harper Perennial, 1998)

Hard Choices for Loving People by Hank Dunn (A&A, 2009)

Hello from Heaven! by Bill and Judy Guggenheim (Bantam, 1997)

Hints on Mediumistic Development by Ursula Roberts (Aquarian Press, 1956)

How to Go On Living When Someone You Love Dies by Therese A. Rando, Ph.D. (Bantam, 1991)

Infinite Quest by John Edward (Sterling Ethos, 2012)

Intuitive Studies by Gordon Smith (Hay House, 2012)

The Jewel in the Lotus by Grace Cooke (White Eagle Publishing Trust, 1973)

Life After Life by Raymond Moody, M.D. (Harpers Paperback, 2001)

The Life Beyond Death by Yogi Ramacharaka (Yogi Publication Society,1909)

Life in Spirit by Harry Edwards (The Healer Publishing, 1976)

Living Images by Coral Polge and Kay Hunter (SAGB, 1997)

Living in Two Worlds by Ursula Roberts (Regency Press, 1984)

Mankind's Latent Powers by Phoebe Payne (Faber & Faber, 1938)

Many Lives, Many Masters by Brian L. Weiss, M.D. (Fireside, 1988)

Mediums and the Development of Mediumship by Rev. Robert G. Chaney (Psychic Books, 1946)

Mediums and Their Work by Linda Williamson (Robert Hale, 1990)

Mediumship Made Simple by Ivy Northage (College of Psychic Studies, 1994)

One Last Time by John Edward (Berkley, 1999)

Parting Visions by Melvin Morse, M.D. (Villard, 1993)

Power of the Soul by John Holland (Hay House, 2007)

The Power of Your Spirit by Stephen O'Brien (Voices, 2003)

Principles of Spiritualism by Lyn de Swarte (Thorsons, 1999)

Psychic Navigator by John Holland (Hay House, 2004)

Second Chance by Suzane Northrop (Amazon Digital Services, 2012)

Spiritual Unfoldment 1 by White Eagle (White Eagle Publishing Trust, 2000)

Spiritual Unfoldment 2 by White Eagle (White Eagle Publishing Trust, 2000)

The Spirit Whisperer by John Holland (Hay House, 2010)

Unknown but Known by Author Ford (Harper & Row, 1968)

Visions, Trips, and Crowded Rooms by David Kessler (Hay House, 2001)

Where Two Worlds Meet by Janet Nohavec and Suzanne Giesemann (Aventine Press, 2011)

You Can Heal Your Heart by Louise Hay and David Kessler (Hay House, 2015)

HELPFUL WEBSITES

After-Death Communication (ADC)
A comprehensive site produced by Bill and Judy Guggenheim, the authors of *Hello From Heaven!* www.after-death.com

AfterLife TV with Bob Olson
The website of Bob Olson, a leading expert on life after death, psychic mediums, after-death communication, past lives, and near-death experiences. He shares interviews with experts, videos of what he's learned from his investigations, and videos of people sharing their afterlife experiences. www.afterlifetv.com

National Spiritualist Association of Churches
Website for the listing of National Spiritualist Association of Churches (NSAC) in the United States. www.nsac.org

ORGANIZATIONS

The following organizations are some that I've worked with or admire, respect, and recommend:

Afterlife Conference
An annual conference dedicated to providing wisdom and support for those dealing with the end of life and bereavement, and also to increase awareness of life beyond the physical body. www.afterlifeconference.com

Afterlife Research and Education Institute
A nonprofit service organization supporting afterlife researchers, developers, educators, and practitioners in their work. www.afterlifeinstitute.org

American Foundation for Suicide Prevention (AFSP)
AFSP raises awareness, funds scientific research, and provides resources and aid to those affected by suicide. www.afsp.org

Association for Research and Enlightenment (A.R.E.)
The official website for Edgar Cayce and for his center in Virginia Beach, VA, that was established over 80 years ago. www.edgarcayce.org

Circles of Wisdom Bookstore
John's favorite bookstore in Andover, MA. A metaphysical bookstore and resource center that does events, readings, and workshops. www.circlesofwisdom.com

Hay House Radio
An inspirational Internet radio station that hosts John's weekly radio show, *Spirit Connections*, as well as many other programs by Hay House authors. www.hayhouseradio.com

Infinity Foundation
Infinity Foundation is Chicago area's leading holistic education center. Infinity offers Courses For Life®, providing experiential courses in personal, professional, and spiritual growth. www.infinityfoundation.org

The Journey Within: Spiritualists' National Union Church
Located in Pompton Lakes, NJ, this recognized Spiritualist Church features many teachers of mediumship and other psychic sciences. Some of the best training can be found here. www.journeywithin.org

Leapin' Lizards

A bookstore and gift shop with two locations in Maine that offers a broad selection of holistic and uplifting merchandise as well as classes, workshops, special events, and psychic readings and healing sessions every day. www.leapinlizards.biz

Lily Dale Assembly

Incorporated in 1879, this meeting place for Spiritualists is located in Lily Dale, NY. The purpose of Lily Dale is to further the science, philosophy, and religion of Spiritualism. Some call this the Mother Ship of spiritualism in the U.S. www.lilydaleassembly.com

Mishka Productions: Celebrate Your Life Events!

Conferences and workshops produced in Sedona, AZ, that feature inspirational speakers and authors who work in the different fields within the body, mind, and spirit. www.mishkaproductions.com

Omega Institute

Located in Rhinebeck, NY, Omega Institute is a nonprofit, mission-driven, and donor-supported educational organization. They're a pioneer in holistic studies helping people and organizations integrate personal growth and social change, moving beyond "the way it is" toward "the way it can be." www.eomega.org

Spirit of Change

Independently published by founding publisher and editor Carol Bedrosian, *Spirit of Change* has grown to become New England's largest free holistic magazine. They also host the fantastic 'New England Natural Living Expo' every year in New England. John says, "It's the *best* expo I've ever been to!" www.spiritofchange.org

U.K. RESOURCES

Arthur Findlay College

Stansted Hall, Stansted Mountfitchet, Essex CM24 8UD, U.K.

The Arthur Findlay College is a residential center where students can study Spiritualist philosophy and religious practice, Spiritualist healing and awareness, spiritual and psychic unfolding, and kindred disciplines. www.arthurfindlaycollege.org

College of Psychic Studies

16 Queensberry Place, London SW7 2EB, U.K.

The College of Psychic Studies (founded in 1884 as the London Spiritualist Alliance) is a nonprofit organization based in South Kensington, London. As one of the oldest establishments of its kind, the nature of their work has evolved to incorporate a more general and widely based exploration of consciousness beyond matter. The core of studies retains a strong focus on the development and understanding of mediumship, psychic ability and healing, as well as the growing capacity of science to explain and explore these phenomena. www.collegeofpsychicstudies.co.uk

Spiritualist Association of Great Britain (SAGB)

11 Belgrave Road, London SW1V 1RB, U.K.

The Spiritualist Association of Great Britain (the SAGB) is a British spiritualist organization. It was established in 1872 and now offers class, workshops, readings, and mediumship demonstrations. www.spiritualistassociation.org.uk

BEREAVEMENT INFORMATION

Bereaved Parents of the USA

A nationwide organization designed to aid and support bereaved parents and their families struggling to overcome their grief after the passing of a child. www.bereavedparentsusa.org

The Compassionate Friends

A nationwide organization of bereaved parents offering friendship, support groups, and one-on-one assistance in your area. www.compassionatefriends.org

Grief.com

A website dedicated to the healing of grief by bereavement expert David Kessler. www.grief.com

HelpGuide

A guide to mental and emotional health for understanding, preventing, and resolving life's challenges. www.helpguide.org/mental /grief_loss.htm

Support After Suicide

The Support After Suicide Community brings together people who are bereaved by suicide. They also provide education and professional development to health, welfare, and education professionals. www.supportaftersuicide.org.au

Wings

Information and inspiration for the bereaved and caregivers, including a quarterly magazine of real stories about people's journeys through grief. www.wingsgrief.org

FURTHER RECOMMENDED ONLINE READING

"Deathbed Visions: Are Dying People Escorted to the Other Side by Loved Ones?" by Stephen Wagner from *ThoughtCo.* www.thoughtco .com/what-we-know-about-deathbed-visions-2594507

"The Different Planes of Existence in the Universe" by Enoch Tan from *Great Genius Insights into Everything* www.greatgenius.com /the-different-planes-of-existence-in-the-universe

"Life After Death? Largest-Ever Study Provides Evidence that 'Out Of Body' and 'Near-Death' Experiences May Be Real" by Adam Withnall from *The Independent* www.independent.co.uk/news/science /life-after-death-largest-ever-study-provides-evidence-that-out-of -body-and-near-death-experiences-9780195.html

"Life Before Birth" by Stephen Wagner from *ThoughtCo.* www.thoughtco.com/life-before-birth-2594548

"Picking Our Parents and Our Life Circumstances" by Erin Pavlina www.erinpavlina.com/blog/2007/05/picking-our-parents-and-our-life -circumstances

"Enhancing the Possibility for a Conscious, Connected and Loving End-Of-Life Experience. Shared Death Experience" from the *Shared Crossing Project* www.sharedcrossing.com/shared-death-experience.html

"The Global Shared Death Experience — Shared Death Study, the Largest Global Shared Death Experience Study" www.shareddeathstudy.org

"What is the Spiritual Self?" from *Caracolores: Awakening Our Inner and Inter-connections* http://caracolores.com/1s-the-individual /what-is-the-spiritual-self

ACKNOWLEDGMENTS

No one ever truly writes a book alone. As they say: "It takes a village!"

Let me first express my appreciation to God, the Universe, Spirit, and, of course, my guides. The guidance and blessings given to me are my deepest treasures, and I hold them close to my heart and my soul. I am eternally blessed and grateful. It's an honor to serve.

To my family, I love you. I wouldn't be who I am without you. Thank you for all the memories we've shared together. I believe that everything can be a learning experience and a catalyst for change.

A special acknowledgment to my mom, who passed away since I wrote my last book. What she and I went through together toward the end of her life was a learning experience that I cherish and wouldn't change for anything! I love you, Jen!

Thank you, Simon Steel, for *all* your support; for your serenity; for your beautiful editing and structure; and, most of all, for helping me create yet another book — one that I hope will inspire many people to develop and grow even further!

To Laura Wooster, thank you for all your help these past couple of years, for your kindness, for your assistance, and most of all . . . for your patience.

I'm truly blessed and forever grateful to have such great people around me. I appreciate all the *special* friends and colleagues that support me while I'm immersed in the process of writing a book. You know *who* you are, and I couldn't get along without your friendship and continued love and support. You have touched my heart and soul forever.

To Louise Hay, all my love and appreciation. Thank you for being one of the best teachers whom I was lucky enough to know and have in my life. I'm sure you're now inspiring the angels on the Other-Side!

To the entire team at Hay House . . . Thank you for your support in all ways, in every department. And a special thank you to Nicolette Salamanca Young for your guidance and editing wisdom.

To the team who runs Hay House Radio, thank you for helping continue to put a little *soul* into my radio show, *Spirit Connections*, for the past 13 years!

To Chris Magruder at Thundering Sky Recording Studios, thank you for your professionalism, kindness, and patience. You rock, Chris!

A special thank you to Cindy Pearlman for your generosity, advice, and wisdom!

Thank you, Ann Hentz, my Tarot Goddess and my co-host once a month on the *Psychic Tarot Hour*. I look forward to every last Monday of the month! May we continue in partnership to help as many people as we can — for as long as we can.

I couldn't finish these acknowledgments without mentioning my beloved dog, Koda. You blessed my life the first day I met you! You continue to teach and remind me each and every day to be present, to be myself, to laugh, and, most importantly, to play!

A special thank you to all those who shared their personal stories for this book. Your story will help and inspire all who read it.

To my students and to *you*, the reader: Thank you for being my ultimate teachers in this lifetime.

And finally, to all the people whom I've been unable to mention: I'm truly blessed by simply knowing you all.

ABOUT THE AUTHOR

John Holland is an internationally renowned psychic medium, spiritual teacher, author, and radio host. His public demonstrations provide audiences with a rare glimpse into the fascinating subject of mediumship, which he delivers in his own unique style, explaining the delicate process of raising his own vibrational energy to link with the Other-Side and deliver messages, which he does with clarity, passion, and the utmost integrity. Having spent two intensive years studying in the U.K., he's subsequently devoted his life to Spirit. He's been working as a psychic medium for over two decades and has become one of the most sought-after professional mediums on the world stage today!

John has starred in several TV specials, including A&E's *Mediums: We See Dead People*, which provided a fascinating insight into how John works as a "psychic time machine," where he's able to pick up vibrations and detailed information from past events, whether it's seen, felt, or heard. He is the author of the best-selling books *Power of the Soul, Psychic Navigator, Born Knowing, The Spirit Whisperer: Chronicles of a Medium*; and the card decks *The Psychic Tarot Oracle Deck, The Psychic Tarot for the Heart*, and *The Spirit Messages: The Daily Guidance Oracle Deck*, all of which are available as apps.

John can be heard every week as he hosts his own Internet radio show, *Spirit Connections*, which has been running for more than 10 years on Hay House Radio.

He's dedicated his life to the ongoing development of his unique gift and sets the barrier high by bringing real integrity to his profession. John says, "If I can help people connect with someone on the Other-Side and bring peace, comfort, and perhaps some closure, then I've done my job."

You can contact the author at:
John Holland
P.O. Box 983, Exeter, NH 03833
(617) 747-4491

www.JohnHolland.com
www.facebook.com/JHollandMedium

Hay House Titles of Related Interest

YOU CAN HEAL YOUR LIFE, the movie, starring Louise Hay & Friends
(available as an online streaming video)
www.hayhouse.com/louise-movie

*THE SHIFT, the movie,*starring Dr. Wayne W. Dyer
(available as an online streaming video)
www.hayhouse.com/the-shift-movie

———————

*The Boy Who Knew Too Much: An Astounding True Story
of a Young Boy's Past-Life Memories,* by Cathy Byrd

*Memories of Heaven: Children's Astounding Recollections of the
Time Before They Came to Earth,* by Dr. Wayne W. Dyer and Dee Garnes

*Mirrors of Time: Using Regression for Physical,
Emotional, and Spiritual Healing,* by Brian L. Weiss, M.D.

*Visions, Trips, and Crowded Rooms:
Who and What You See Before You Die,* by David Kessler

*You Can Heal Your Heart: Finding Peace After
a Breakup, Divorce, or Death,* by Louise Hay and David Kessler

*Your Life After Their Death:
A Medium's Guide to Healing After a Loss,* by Karen Noé

All of the above are available at your local bookstore,
or may be ordered by contacting Hay House (see next page).

———————

We hope you enjoyed this Hay House book. If you'd like to receive our online catalog featuring additional information on Hay House books and products, or if you'd like to find out more about the Hay Foundation, please contact:

Hay House LLC, P.O. Box 5100, Carlsbad, CA 92018-5100
(760) 431-7695 or (800) 654-5126
www.hayhouse.com® • www.hayfoundation.org

———

Published in Australia by:
Hay House Australia Publishing Pty Ltd
18/36 Ralph St., Alexandria NSW 2015
Phone: +61 (02) 9669 4299
www.hayhouse.com.au

Published in the United Kingdom by:
Hay House UK Ltd
The Sixth Floor, Watson House,
54 Baker Street, London W1U 7BU
Phone: +44 (0) 203 927 7290
www.hayhouse.co.uk

Published in India by:
Hay House Publishers (India) Pvt Ltd
Muskaan Complex, Plot No. 3,
B-2, Vasant Kunj, New Delhi 110 070
Phone: +91 11 41761620
www.hayhouse.co.in

———

Access New Knowledge.
Anytime. Anywhere.

Learn and evolve at your own pace
with the world's leading experts.

www.hayhouseU.com